Talking to Animals

Books by the same author

Dog Training My Way
The Book of Ponies
The A to Z of Dogs and Puppies
Talking in Spanish
Talking in French
Talking in German
Talking in Italian

Talking to Animals

Barbara Woodhouse

'Lord, if I had always such a nice, attentive person to
listen to me as you are, I could go on talking
about horses to the end of time.'
The Romany Rye

Fontana/Collins

First published 1954
First published in Fontana 1974

© Copyright Barbara Woodhouse 1954

Made and printed in Great Britain by
William Collins Sons & Co Ltd Glasgow

to my husband

*whose understanding of my love for animals
made this book possible*

contents

	Preface	11
1	I should have been born in a Stable	15
2	Archie, Alouette, and Adoring Dogs	26
3	Not quite at home on the Range	35
4	Horse-breaking without Fears	58
5	Taming Horses in the Argentine	68
6	South-American Jean	76
7	Horse-dealing Housewife	85
8	A Farm in a Town	94
9	Conversation Farm	106
10	Life on twelve broad Acres	120
11	A real Farm at last	137
12	Jyntee and Juno – Career Dogs	145
13	Discoursing with Animal Film-stars	156
14	The Dogs and I train the Dog-trainers	168
15	Snow Queen: Film-star among Cows	176
16	Talking to your own Animals	180

illustrations

Between pages 64 and 65
Approaching an unbroken pony, breathing gently down my
nostrils
The pony approaches me
The 'How do you do'
Friends
The pony meets a shoe for the first time
Off we go, hold tight!
The breathing 'How do you do' works with cattle too

Between pages 128 and 129
Junia and our kittens
Untrained dogs after six hours training on a weekend course
Patrick, Judith and Chica, Queenie and Snow Queen, Juno and
I await Master's return home
The Author at home with her pets
Aubretia gets a kiss
Reared in the hot cupboard, he thought he was human
Junia and the baby chickens
Nanny takes care of Queenie's twins; Patrick and Juno help

preface

I believe that animals have been talking to human beings ever since we were all made and put into this world 'for mutual society, help, and comfort, both in prosperity and adversity', to quote from the marriage service; and that if we human beings have been unbelievably slow in taking advantage of the gifts we have been offered, we have nobody but ourselves to blame. And I feel that, as animals are so much quicker in picking up our thoughts and words than we are in picking up theirs, they must have a very poor opinion of the intelligence of the human race.

This is not to deny that in every race and in every age there have always been individuals known for their love and understanding of the animal kingdom, who have forged indestructible bonds of friendship with the animal world. Most of us have read, with absorbed interest, of people like Tom Faggus and his strawberry mare, or Prince Llewellyn whose faith in his dog failed him in a crisis. Practically everyone knows of someone who has a 'way with animals' and who seems able to communicate moods, notions and sympathies, with or without using words, to animal friends. Those people are indeed blessed, for their lives are a fulfilment and an example of what we would like to see happening among the human races. But I fear that with human beings the hates of the many overcome the love of the few. So few animals hate, and so many millions of them wait to give to someone or other the love and submission they long to show to a master!

How is it possible to learn how to talk to animals? I think one has to have an intense love of them, and an inborn conviction that they are eager to comply with our wishes, if we can just show them how. Looking back, it seems to me that there has never in my life been a misunderstanding with an animal that has not been capable of being straightened out for our mutual well-being. So much of my communication with animals is wordless, words as such meaning nothing to animals, being simply carriers of tone. It is our way of employing words that matters. We could use the same words to praise, to scold, to encourage, and to excite, if we had enough command of our intonations to make each usage different; but how many people can do this? Very few. Therefore, in their contact with animals many have to try to teach them the actual meaning of words, and this must of necessity be a very slow business.

Patience is a vital quality in dealing with animals: lose your temper with an animal and you have built up a barrier that will have to be slowly broken down again before mutual trust and confidence is restored. But I do not mean by this that one should never give the impression of having lost one's temper, for I firmly believe that occasionally an animal has to be very severely spoken to for misbehaviour, but that severity must be 'put on'. It must not be a genuinely lost temper. When you put it on, you can take it off again, and bring back the loving tone immediately; the animal knows the difference and is ready and waiting to be loved again should he mend his ways.

Animals often 'play up' their owners. One so often sees lapdogs which are completely impervious to honeyed talk, but which respond immediately to sensible commands. There are few animals that cannot distinguish the sharp edge of the usually placid voice which reminds them that it is at that moment better to obey. I do not believe that all animals are born good, nor do I believe that one can reform all wrong-doers. As in the human race, we have rogues, and unless one has endless time to spend on these rogues perhaps one would be better engaged in teaching the right-minded animals. However, I personally love the bad animals. They are a challenge to my spirit, and if I had the time I would concentrate a great deal more on the rogues, dogs especially. The animals that need my help and sympathy are the frightened ones, the misunderstood ones, the ones with the wrong owners, and the bad ones. But to carry out this work would mean separating most of the animals from their owners and never returning them, for in nine cases out of ten it is the human being who is at fault. So, when readers first try talking to animals I advocate confining their activities to the normal animals, sound in heart and mind, leaving a few of us only to deal with the really bad ones.

I often think that I must be one of the very luckiest of women in having a family who all share my intense love of animals. My husband, before he was inspired with my own enthusiasm, had had very little to do with livestock. Yet from the very first he joined me in all my interests, and very soon became a humble slave of the animal kingdom, just as I am. It is he who so willingly performs the thankless task of cleaning sheds, and fetching and carrying, and without the rewards that I enjoy: the sense of achievement when my cows produce high yields, the satisfaction of taming a horse. Times without number he had stayed at home so as to be with our animals, when we have had no one else to leave in the house and I myself have had to fulfil an engagement: a real sacrifice, as normally we only enjoy things when we are together. Never once in my life have I known any member of my family to grumble if we have had to cancel some outing because an animal has needed my care; for they all know and understand that I could never relax and enjoy anything if I was worrying over one of our creatures. I think the most difficult thing that my husband has to endure is my insistence that I milk my cows, or perhaps help to calve one of them myself, when I am unwell. For being a doctor he knows the risk I am taking; nevertheless we both see that it is best that way. Life without risk is not a fulfilment of our destinies, and I am sure that my own destiny is to devote myself to my family which, by the consent of all its human members, includes all our animals and recognizes their claim to equal love and care.

> There is in souls a sympathy in sounds;
> And as the mind is pitched, the ear is pleased
> With melting airs, or martial, brisk, or grave;
> Some chord in unison with what we hear
> Is touched within us, and the heart replies.
>
> COWPER

1   *I should have been born in a Stable*

I often think I should have been happier born in a stable than at St Columba's College, Rathfarnham, where I first saw the light of day in May 1910. The college nestled in the shelter of the Wicklow Mountains, with a glorious view stretching down to Dublin Bay, wild and windswept in winter, and sheltered only from the north by a park and huge woods. I always remember the beauty of the park because I used to be put to rest in summer on a camp bed under a huge cypress tree, where only iron railings separated me from it. There were deer in plenty roaming the woods and park, and if I lay very still they would come up to the fence, their beautiful noses sniffing the air, and their ears fluttering backwards and forwards as if they had a telegraph system and were telling the rest of the herd that it was quite safe to come and have a look at this human child. Often I used to creep off my bed and sit beside the fence, to wait for the buck to come and see if I was endangering his wives. I used to stroke his velvety nose and talk sweet nothings to him, for I already lived in my mind in the world of animals. It always amazed me with what speed they all disappeared when they were frightened, their little spindly legs seeming too thin to leap and fly over the hillocks in the park. Within seconds there wasn't one to be seen. They learnt to take bread from me, and many tit-bits from my tea and breakfast found their way into my pinafore pockets.

When it was warm, we used to sit on the wide steps that led up to the College entrance, and Mother's pet fantail pigeons, red, blue, and white, would fly down to fuss around us. They were all very tame for she loved all birds and animals and these were her particular hobby. She used to show me how a specially-good bird's tail really was shaped in a wide fan, and how his head reached right back to his tail, and I always felt they must get very giddy leaning back all the time. Mother's other hobby was rabbits, and she used to have hundreds of them, mostly beautiful red Belgian hares and soft blue beverens. At an early age I was given two Dutch rabbits for my own, and I used to spend hours brushing their fur and cleaning their hutch. But, alas, one day someone stole them, and that was the first time in my life that I felt as if my heart were broken. I was given some other rabbits to console me, but it was never quite the same again.

Early in the First World War, when I was four years old, soldiers were billeted on us and their horses turned out in the park. My Nannie tells me that I perpetually escaped from her watchful eye, and was often to be found surrounded by enormous horses eating tit-bits of grass that I picked for them, after I had squeezed myself through the railings of the park to be among them. But one day when they missed me I was found sitting on the back of the pony that was kept for the governess cart. I was trying vainly to put its collar on over its head by edging myself up its neck as I held the collar. How on earth I ever climbed up with that heavy collar I do not know. From that day stable doors had to be locked against me, for I used to sit between the legs of the enormous carthorses belonging to the farm attached to the school, and that, to my nurse, looked far too dangerous.

Every afternoon we used to be sent out for a drive in the pony trap. I've often heard my mother say that it was 'weather only fit for the children', and sometimes with the rain coming down, or the icy winds blowing a gale, it was a miracle that we didn't all catch pneumonia – but in those days it was thought that children should have fresh air no matter what the weather. The pony used to be brought round to the door at two o'clock sharp, and I used always to go and give it a piece of sugar. It seemed to find it difficult to eat this with its bit in, but I found that if I put the sugar into its mouth at one side it could chew it straight away between its back teeth. This used to make the groom very angry with me, for the beautifully burnished bit would become all frothy and sticky, and there weren't any chromium-plated ones in those days. Riding in the pony trap was heaven to me and at a very early age Nanny used to let me take the reins. I well remember that, when I was about five, we had a governess who used to come every day from Dublin to our nearest station, Dundrum, which was five miles from the College. My greatest joy then was to go and meet her in the pony trap quite alone. I must say I had a wonderful mother not to worry when her tiny little girl went away all alone for such a distance. I know there was no traffic to speak of then, but I don't think I would have trusted any child of mine quite like that. But Mother never seemed to worry over my dealings with animals, for she had great faith in them. I never remember being told not to talk to a vicious horse, or not to touch a dog, and we constantly had animals of every kind suffering from a variety of injuries and complaints in our nursery. A hedgehog used to give us tremendous fun by hiding under Nanny's chair, where sometimes, after having been up all night with my baby sister, she would fall asleep by the fire after lunch. She was doing this one day, when the hedgehog, who had been sleeping under her chair, suddenly decided to go exploring. Slowly he crept up Nanny's foot and began to crawl up her leg, when she awoke with an unearthly yell, much to our amusement. I remember a visitor coming to the College one day and stopping to talk to me; I was fascinated by his tales of the farm he ran, and he for his part was amused by my interest and he asked me if I'd like a baby pig for my own. Naturally I said 'yes', but without thinking where its home would be. I persuaded Nanny to drive over to the farm to see my pig, one of a litter of twelve from which I could have my choice. Of course I chose the tiniest of all, the most pathetic little runt, and nothing could persuade me to take a bigger one. I christened it Pinky and home it came. We soon discovered that it was really far too weak to have left its mother, but we wrapped it up in cotton wool and put it to bed hopefully by the nursery fire. It fed beautifully from a bottle, and used to squeal with excitement when its feeding time drew near. Poor Pinky had been used to feeds during the night, and although Nanny did get up at midnight to give it a bottle, it got out of its box unbeknown to us one night and caught a bad chill. All the care in the world couldn't have saved it, for we had no penicillin in those days, and it died of pneumonia. And that was the second tragedy of my young life.

We had a corner of the nursery made safe for our extraordinary collection of pets, and a lamb and a duck with a broken wing, whom we nicknamed Beaky Bar (why, I can't think), joined our household. Tiny rabbits with no mother, injured birds, sick baby turkeys, and a tiny little Pomeranian dog, all came under our loving care. They were all kept spotlessly clean, and they slept at night in their special cages or boxes. We never had the normal pets that most children keep, like mice or tortoises, although my eldest sister once had some guinea pigs. She became quite an accomplished breeder after a time and used to make quite a lot of pocket money with them. But I never made any money out of my own pets, for tragedy after tragedy seemed to befall them. Rats, alas, stole all my baby rabbits, my poor old donkey died of old age, and Sandy, our collie, became a sheep-killer. One of my greatest weekly treats was to take bread and carrots and sugar and go down with my mother to see all the horses in the farm stables. Great shire horses used to lean out of their boxes, and although they could have nipped off my tiny hand in one bite, they gently played about it with their lips until they had taken my offerings safely into their mouths. There was one particularly bad-tempered horse that had to be kept right at the end, because it used to bite everyone who passed, but he became my special favourite and reminded me of Ginger in *Black Beauty*, my favourite book. He always had more sugar from me than all the others. Next on my list was a huge black shire horse with a white blaze down his face and a lovely tuft of hair on his upper lip, which hung down four or five inches and made him look very funny eating sugar, just as if he had a moustache wagging about.

So I passed my early childhood. When I was nine, my father died and we moved to Brighton, where our dreary house in a square made no provision for animals. I made up for this by treasuring every book about animals I could lay my hands on. Every milkman's pony was mine in thought for the few minutes during which I could fondle it. Once some big horses attached to a removal van stood in the road outside our house, one of them wearing a muzzle. I put my small hand inside the muzzle to caress the horse and gave it sugar. He was completely gentle with me, but I got a severe scolding from the driver when he came out, on account of the risk I had run. To me that seemed nonsense, as I loved the horse and I knew he would not bite me.

Such a declaration of faith of course only incensed the driver, as all such naïve statements of belief have offended the wary since time began. I was too young then to prattle of affinities and creative thought, or to try to explain the almost inexplicable. All I could have told him was that the muzzle was not necessary for my protection. But I think I knew that mentioning such things to grown-ups was pointless, and that so long as the horse and I understood one another, there was nothing to worry about.

When I was thirteen we moved from the dreariness of the Brighton square to a lovely old house at Oxford. To me it was near heaven! There were outhouses and stables, which of course my imagination at once filled with animals.

I had always wanted to have a pony but had never possessed the money to buy one. My second wish was for a goat, and I studied all available books on 'Goat-keeping on Money-making Lines' until I felt that there was very little left that I didn't know about goats. In a rash moment I wrote, for a magazine, an article with the title, 'Goat-keeping for Children as Pets'. It was accepted by the editor and those first few pennies I earned were put aside to buy a goat. Christmas, with its half-crown tips from aunts and uncles, followed an autumn when I had made three whole pounds by picking and selling fruit, and at last I had five pounds, which I knew to be the price of a goat. Proudly I went to a goat farm and chose a beautiful black-and-white one. I paid my money and they said they would send her on to me. When the goat arrived, however, it wasn't the one I had chosen, but a much inferior one, which I let them know at once – but only to be laughed to scorn. I was told that the goat I thought I had chosen would have cost at least ten pounds! So I had been cheated in my very first venture, and it made me bitter; but, in spite of the fact that the goat I had got was not nearly as good as the one I had chosen, I decided to make up for its deficiencies by doing everything in my power to help her to give plenty of milk as soon as her kids arrived. I did not know yet how to milk, but I had so carefully studied the diagrams in the goat book that I felt sure I could do it without any lessons. My little goat gave birth to three kids, and the happy event supplied my first study of nature and its wonderful ways. When I came to milk her, I sat down to do it from behind, for there seemed a big expanse of udder there, and the book of words had said nothing about where to sit. In a few minutes I had mastered the technique, but I didn't seem to be getting very much milk, and I supposed the kids were drinking it all. I very proudly took the milk into the house to the rest of the family, thinking they would be longing to taste its delicious flavour, as all the books had said that it was most palatable.

But, alas, my sister and brothers took one sip each and then spat it all out. I drank some myself, and would dearly have liked to do the same, for I don't think I had ever tasted anything nastier, although I wasn't going to admit it. I kept goats for three years and always drank their milk, rather than say that I didn't like it, but I never got really reconciled to its flavour. I brought up my kids and sold them, and then bought another goat, a really nice one, and sold the milk to T.B. patients in the district.

My brother and I often quarrelled, and one day when I wanted to go up some stairs that he was painting, he said I couldn't. Nevertheless I did, but he paid me out later by painting all the white parts of my beloved goat a bright green. I shall never forget it to my dying day. I wept buckets of tears, for nothing I could do would get the paint off, and it didn't finally disappear until the poor thing shed her coat. What horrid beasts some boys can be!

It was about this time that Mother bought two young heifers to eat down the orchard grass, my goats not being allowed in there as they ate the apple trees. When these heifers were about fifteen months old and I still hadn't my heart's desire of owning a pony, I decided I would break in one of the heifers to be ridden. The light roan one was my choice and I found her extremely amenable. In no time she was wearing a head-collar, with two reins on it at the sides, and a saddle. She didn't seem to object at all when I first climbed onto her back. She felt quite different from a pony, in so much as she was low in front, and when she trotted I was thrown slightly forward, but I soon got used to that. I taught her to canter and stop easily, and very shortly, when young school friends came to see me, I used to allow them also to ride her. I wanted to go a step further with her, so I erected some hurdles and taught her to jump. She needed little teaching in actual fact, for cattle can jump just as easily as horses. I had to lean back on landing, or I should have fallen over her head; the lack of 'front' made it difficult to stay on if I leant forward. I taught her with a low bar first of all, and then a hurdle, and finally put a bar up above the hurdle. I wanted to go hunting on her, but Mother wouldn't let me, although I rode her all around the roads just like a pony. I used to ride her often, and to me she was every bit as good as a pony.

I think any quiet well-handled steer or heifer could be safely ridden with a little breaking in, and my own children have always ridden my cows, which seem to enjoy taking them round the fields. My small son has often ridden even my big bull. He would go down the road daily to bring the milking herd up, always climbing onto the back of one of the cows to ride it home.

I am now jumping ahead a few years, but as readers may already have caught sight of the picture showing Patrick enjoying his cow-back ride, I may as well describe how this came about, for I would not for one moment suggest that any child, however fearless, should be encouraged to emulate my little boy with just any cow, however tractable, unless the advice I give receives careful attention.

My bull had been handled gently from birth and was never penned – penned bulls have only their own lonely thoughts to occupy them. He had known only love and kindness all his life. We usually turned him into a field from which he could see his wives. I myself saw to his cleanliness, his grooming, his food. Of course I had often breathed my affection for him up his nostrils – a trick that I learnt in the Argentine, as will be told later – and my children were always with me when I took him to and from his grazing. They liked riding on his back and I was always with them, but a bull, however gentle, must never be deemed as trustworthy as a cow. His nature can never be as placid, and a day may come when his upbringing counts for nothing against the irritation caused by a stray dog crossing his path and perhaps nipping his heels.

Bulls have been ridden in the past and will no doubt be

ridden in the future, and I myself have never had a bad-tempered or a difficult bull, but I should always expect to be on the alert to see that nothing happened to disillusion either of us.

Slowly my bank balance rose as I sold my goats' milk and their kids, and at last I had enough money to buy a pony. I bought a twenty-seven-year-old one that had come originally from Wyoming. I had first seen this old pony six months earlier, when it was being ridden by its master in full cowboy rigout in a fancy dress parade and carnival held at Porthleven in Cornwall, where I was staying for our summer holidays. I had to go and talk to it, and its owner told me he was going to sell it. Without thought about how I was going to pay for it, I asked him to sell me the horse and to keep him until I had the money. I also wrote him a formal letter, putting my offer in writing in a most businesslike way, though what its legal value was from one so young I just don't know. I knew poor old Tommy just had to be mine; his wretched thin body and dipped back were an open sesame to my heart. Even the nine pounds asked for him was really a sum beyond my purse, but I don't think I would have taken a more beautiful animal even if I had been offered it, so long as this pathetic old bag of bones needed a loving owner to comfort him in his old age. I believed that my great love would revive his worn-out spirit, and that his shaggy coat would become like ebony under my care. Together we would live in a world of our own, where he would be my fairy prince in disguise. Always in my life the most wretched and miserable of animals have been the ones I have invariably wanted and later owned. I have never coveted show horses or cattle or dogs, although many of my animals, after the loving care I have bestowed on them, have won in the show ring, owing purely to their superb manners or performance in some sphere or other. So Tommy became my very own some months after I had first decided to buy him. My heart was so full that I could hardly bear to leave him, ugly and old though he was. To me he was everything that a horse should be, and I spent hours grooming him and teaching him tricks. I taught him one trick that I regretted: it was to climb a ladder, having three-inch-wide steps, up into the stable loft. But alas, I had not taught him to get down again from that height, which I am sure would in any case have been impossible, so I had to get the milkman to bring about twenty trusses of straw and it was on that that he finally climbed down. That pony became almost human. We lived in a world of our own, played cowboys and Indians together, and the pony knew when to lie down for me to hide behind him and shoot Red Indians. He learnt also to do all the tricks I saw in a circus, such as walking on his hind legs, counting, and many other things. I never wanted another pony, and it wasn't until he died at a very ripe old age that I had any other.

People may wonder how it was possible to teach an old pony of twenty-seven years all the things I did teach him, but to me it was natural that he should want to learn. I was the first person for many a year who had treated him as a friend and not as a slave, the terms on which most cow-ponies are employed. I used every form of encouragement, including bribery with sugar; I used love, enthusiasm and will-power, and of course the telepathic communication without which I could never talk to animals at all. I don't pretend that Tommy knew we were supposed to be chasing Indians – all he knew was that his mistress was happy when he flew up and down the hills as if the devil were after him, and her happiness was easily known through the touch of her fingers and the laugh in her voice.

That is what animals go by, the spirit of their owner, her moods, her happiness or her unhappiness. If one has a bond with animals they want to join in one's life as much as they can, and they learn to pick up one's moods. Tommy knew all mine, I know. I have laughed with him, rejoiced with him over successes I have had, and I have cried into his mane over some unhappiness that only he would understand. There are so many things we can tell our animals that we cannot confide to human beings for fear of being sneered at or simply not believed. That is why I believe lonely people get great comfort from having an animal to tell their thoughts to. I used to spend all my free time with Tommy, often just sitting quietly in a corner of his stable watching his poor old tummy swell as I gave him more and more food in the hope that it would fatten him. I could hardly bear to go to bed at night and leave him to his loneliness. Mother used to ask me if I ever spoke or thought of anything else but Tommy, and quite honestly, I don't think I did!

2 Archie, Alouette, and Adoring Dogs

I left school at the early age of sixteen, never having learnt anything there that in my opinion could later be of the slightest good to me. Every mistress had hated me because I always went to school smelling strongly of horse. I now felt it was high time to go and do something I wanted to do, so I sold my goats and turned my pony out to grass, and after badgering my mother nearly to insanity was sent off to an Agricultural College. It was not thought proper in those days for girls to learn agriculture as they do today, so it happened that I was the only girl on that side of the establishment. But I had spent the first nine years of my life in a boys' public school, so it seemed quite natural to me to continue to work without others of my own sex. I was in my element at college. I milked the cows with a great love for them, and found that I only had to milk a cow myself for its yield to go up. We all had farm duties to carry out, and the cunning men would not always do theirs, so I think I milked most of the cows morning and night for three years. I loved it and they hated it, so why not! I loved every minute of my time there, and turned out to have a few brains and got quite good reports instead of the bad ones I'd had at school.

But I missed my dog and my pony, so I found a cottager nearby who could keep my dog for me; and the next term I brought her back with me, and as soon as my work was over I was out with her. Then I succeeded in getting on the right side of the cowman and the farm bailiff, and my pony joined me in a paddock behind the cowshed. Phew, was there a row when I was eventually found out! I felt it was stupid, since we were all obviously mad on animals, and I couldn't understand why we should be denied them. I spent many hours looking after the sheep, and I learnt a lot from the old shepherd who loved his sheep as I did. I didn't think they were the stupid creatures they were supposed to be, for when they got fly-blown they used to wait so sensibly to be caught and treated, and 'my sheep', as I liked to call them, would come racing over to me if they heard my footsteps in the road. At lambing time I suffered with the ewes. They seemed to have a particularly bad time of it, and I was not at all sure that Mother Nature was a very kind person to know.

At the end of my training I gained the second highest marks in the college and was offered a temporary job experimenting on 'Which foods tainted milk, and why'. I had twelve cows given to me to experiment with, and three other Universities and Colleges, as well as my own, were working on what the Ministry of Agriculture particularly wanted to find out: namely, why and how sugar beet pulp tainted the milk. After having tried everything I could think of, but still without any positive result, I got up one night at midnight and milked my cows. I found that the milk was badly tainted, but that by the following morning the taint had gone. What I had discovered was that it was the time factor in the case that really mattered, and it was a short step to finding out the quantities and the actual time it took for this sugar beet pulp to taint the milk. I proudly claimed to have solved their problem, and hoped for thanks and an increase in my pay. But all that I got was the sack! For, although the original grant was for one year, and they had thought it would take as long as that to find this thing out, I had stupidly made my discovery in just three months. Ministries have no hearts. I had to leave college, and I went home to Oxford.

One day soon afterwards I went to the Oxford cattle market and saw a darling little pony there, but one, it appeared, that had an appalling reputation. I heard that two professional breakers had given her up as hopelessly wicked, and in disgrace she was to be sold without a character. But I loved her at first sight and I waited anxiously for the time of the sale to come. I started the bidding at fifteen shillings, and then someone bid a pound, but when I said thirty shillings she became mine.

I walked her the three miles home, and started at once to teach her to carry a sack on her back. I kept dropping the sack off her, and every time I did this I made her stop. She soon began to learn, and it was not long before I got on her back to find that my legs nearly reached to the ground. I hadn't a saddle for her, and she had no shoulder to sit behind as a bigger animal would have had, so when she lowered her head and bucked, off I went at once, only to land neatly with my own legs round her front legs, although I still held onto the reins. She stood back violently and threw her head to one side. Poor little girl, I could see that she had done this often before and had been hit over the head. I got up from the ground and with soothing words offered her some sugar. She took this rather diffidently, as if she waited for a blow to fall. But after some minutes, and still speaking softly all the time, I got on her back again and urged her into a walk. She bucked again, though now with far less vigour. Nevertheless, I was again unseated. This time, however, my legs stayed round her neck, as did my arms, and there I clung like grim death. The weight of me made it impossible for her to do anything, and after a few seconds she gave up. I then stood up and caressed her again and fed her with more sugar. Once more I mounted, fervently wishing I had a small enough saddle for her, but she now went like a lamb, and in no time at all we were trotting happily round the orchard. I called her Alouette.

It was shortly after she came into my possession that I was offered a job by relatives to look after their garden and to be a companion to my deaf aunt. As I had not yet made up my mind what to do with myself, I said I would go and see how we got on. It did not strike me as the ideal job, since animals, not gardening, were my abiding passion, but my aunt had promised that if we got on well together she might buy a farm for me to run.

I left my little Alouette in my mother's care in the orchard at home, and went off to try out the job. At first I missed my pony terribly and spent much of my free time trying to find somewhere I could keep her if I got permission to have her with me. In the end I went and saw the Colonel of the army barracks nearby, who was a kindly man and obviously a horse lover. He said he knew it would be breaking all regulations, but Alouette could have a spare loosebox in the army stables. He told me to keep quiet about it and, if the General should come on an inspection, to take her away quickly. I was immensely grateful, and I asked my aunt for a free week-end to go home to Oxford to fetch her.

When I got her she looked very funny in the army loosebox bedded up to her knees in straw! The big army horses on either side seemed fascinated by her dainty beauty, and the army grooms spoilt her all day long. I used to ride her very early in the morning, when no one was about, and this soon got me into trouble, for I saw a lovely big unfenced green field, where we went at once and raced happily about. A few days afterwards, when I got home for breakfast, my uncle, looking extremely angry, showed me a letter, a very angry letter, from the manager of a seed farm, who said he understood that it was my pony and me who had been using their trial grass plots as an exercising ground, and that if I did it again they would sue me for damages. How on earth could I have known that it was a trial ground! It had looked quite an ordinary field of grass to me, but I realized that I must go round at once to their head office to apologize, and as Alouette and I were the joint culprits, I felt that she should come too. I found the office in a big converted country house, and on arriving knocked and asked for the manager. I was told that his office was on the second floor, and my informants were more than surprised when they saw me with a pony and I assured them that we were both going upstairs to see the manager. And, with a soft word or two to Alouette, up the stairs we went, knocked on the door, and went in. I don't think I have ever seen anyone more surprised than the manager was then, and his secretary at once fled for her life. However, after humble apologies from both of us, we were forgiven, and we went down again the way we had come. If the manager ever reads this, I wonder if he will remember the incident?

I never became happy in my gardening work, for I was a wild creature longing to spread my wings, and it all bored me stiff. I felt quite sorry for the funny little Yorkshire terrier, whom I had to brush and comb every morning as one of my tasks. I used to take him away out into the country, and in spite of his silky coat we used to go hunting the wonderful unknown scents of the hedgerows. Although only weighing about three pounds and hampered by a long coat and a bow, he was the most sporting little person imaginable, and we both used to return to our rather dull routine much refreshed by our rambles.

After a while I decided to return home, so Alouette and I said goodbye to our good friends at the barracks and to my kind and well-meaning aunt, and we went away to seek further adventures.

At home again, I decided to teach children riding on Alouette, who was now completely safe to ride, and pupils soon flowed in. I used to run miles and miles with them, and more and more kept coming to my school, so I soon had enough money to buy a horse for myself, which I now needed badly, since I had too many pupils to run with any more. I asked a local horse dealer how much a horse would cost; he said he had just the thing for me, an old one that had been the leader on an Oxford to London coach. The poor thing had been shot through the lung in the war, and now had only one lung, but was otherwise sound in the wind and capable of work. I got a vet. to look at him for me and then bought him for sixteen pounds. So Archie now joined my family, and as I had named my little pony Alouette, the two A's went rather well together.

Archie was the cleverest old boy possible. He was sixteen hands and up to great weight. Yet he would carry the tiniest mite round my riding-school orchard with the greatest care, and if I said 'Archie, canter at the third tree', he would do exactly as I told him.[1] It was a big orchard, so I trained him to go round it once with whatever order I gave and then always to come back for further instructions. I never shouted at my pupils or at him either, but just told them quietly what they had done wrong, and then what to do next.

Some time later, when I had increased my stable to four horses and now hired them out, a very smart-looking young undergraduate, in impeccable white breeches, came to hire a horse. My rule was never to let a horse out until I was sure the person who wanted to hire him could ride properly and was not likely to injure or ill-treat him, so, when this young man came to see me, I asked him to come into the riding school to ride Archie a few times round to see how he got on. At this he was most annoyed and claimed that he could ride well. So I replied that in that case he wouldn't mind giving me a show of what he could do. I could see Archie almost laugh as he came into the orchard, a silent laugh, and I knew that the old villain was already planning what to do with him. The beautiful young man had great difficulty in mounting the horse owing to the tight breeches that he wore, but with an effort he succeeded. Archie then trotted gently to the one corner of the orchard where there was a large patch of nettles, and immediately gave a terrific buck. Off went his lordship

[1] I must ask the reader to turn to the last chapter for more explicit information on my method of helping Archie to achieve this result (see page 189).

straight into the nettles! As I went to his rescue, Archie trotted off, kicking up his heels, with tail and head held high, a thing I'd never seen him do before. I helped the crestfallen young man to get up, his face a mass of stings, and took him indoors to apply a simple remedy. His riding for that day was over, he decided.

My riding school grew and grew until I had fifteen horses. They were a very good lot, and I took enormous pride in looking after them myself. I used to start lessons at seven, which seemed to be a favourite time for the undergraduates to come, and in summer I would give a one hour's lesson before breakfast. I used to suffer tortures wondering whether my patrons would treat their horses properly, and I compiled a black list of those who dared to bring them back hot. By doing this I got a reputation for being rather fierce, and many an undergraduate has certainly been made to walk his horse for half an hour after bringing it home. But they knew that they got first-class horses to ride and for that reason I never lacked customers.

During term time I was usually exceptionally busy, but during the vacations the horses got a well-earned rest, and I kept in only five of them each week for riding; the others were just lightly exercised or turned out to grass in the summer. It was during these slack times that I had the idea of boarding dogs, so I put up a notice one day on our fence, and almost at once dog-owners came to enquire. I felt it would be a very happy occupation to take in dogs that might fret when their owners went away, and to give them as much as possible of home comfort. I had no kennels, but only the looseboxes vacated by the resting horses, so I put five dogs into each loosebox, taking the greatest care each time to choose dogs that I thought would get on well together and be good companions to each other. I always asked first if a dog was a fighter, and if so I kept it separately.

I felt myself to be very much in my element, morning and night, when I had the whole lot of them out playing together in the orchard. Sometimes there were as many as forty together, and people used to peep over the fence to watch this lovely sight. The dogs played together quite happily, and waited most obediently to be taken back to their stables. Naturally I had to train them with great firmness when they first came, as few of them knew what the word 'No' meant, but I loved them all equally from the moment they came and they all knew it. Sometimes one of them would bark or howl at night out of loneliness, but at the first whimper, if I heard it, I would get up to soothe it

Occasionally a new one would really pine; then he or she came into my bedroom, and one night I had eleven of them in my room. Luckily it was a big room, but as I fell asleep I felt myself being watched tenderly by twenty-two eyes. They never made a sound in the night or disturbed me at all, but, alas, the seeds of possible trouble were sown, for of course this constant companionship was what all the dogs longed for above all else. The result was that when their owners arrived to take them home, and were given a rather perfunctory welcome, they were sometimes more than a little annoyed – and worse was to come. For one morning after the end of the first fortnight's holiday in August, which was always my busiest time, I got up in the morning and looked out of my window to find there, patiently awaiting my appearance, twenty-three of my ex-boarders, including one dog from Banbury which was twenty miles or so away. Soon telephone calls came pouring in: 'Was Bruce with me?' 'Yes, Bruce was,' and so on, and the irritated owners arrived one by one to fetch their dogs again, and to take them home, and on my advice to keep them shut up afterwards just for a day or two.

The dog from Banbury returned to me three days running, and the infuriated owner accused me of stealing his dog's affections. I felt rather hurt by the fury of these despised owners, for I had felt that in making the dogs happy I had been doing the right thing. But apparently one mustn't make them *too* happy!

I taught most of my boarders good manners, and I had only two really bad fights during the whole three years that I boarded dogs, and even those dogs learnt to agree after a few days with me. I believe that all animals can live together in peace, and they certainly seemed to pick up the happy atmosphere after a few days. But, alas, dogs kept coming back to me, and owners used to ring me up to ask if I would take their dogs as a present since they were no longer any use or pleasure to them. And this now happened so often that I was forced reluctantly to give up taking any more boarders at all.

It was shortly after this that I was invited to go out to the Argentine to stay with some friends. This greatly appealed to me, so I sold my riding school as a going concern, pensioned off Archie and Alouette, and set sail for adventure. But it was to a life rather different from what I had expected; for soon after my arrival my elderly host lost his wife, and it was upon me that the main task of running his house depended for some time after.

3   Not quite at home
on the Range

When I set sail from England for South America in the early 1930's, I am sure that I had in me more of the pioneering spirit than even Columbus himself. I was going out to a country that I knew little about, except from the wonderful books of W. H. Hudson and R. B. Cunninghame-Graham. I had been warned that the *estancia*[1] to which I had been invited had none of the comforts of an English home, and that there was no wireless there, or telephones, or anything of that kind, but that only thrilled me all the more. There were, of course, vivid pictures in my mind from the innumerable cowboy films that I had seen and my mind's eye pictured stalwart men with six-shooters, and the inevitable cattle rustlers – but that was all the background that I had.

I travelled out on a cargo boat which took a whole month to reach Buenos Aires, and I soon decided that riding the waves was not one of my strong points, for the smell of the engines in our small ship, the constant vibration, and the indescribably horrible odour of the disinfectant blocks that hung everywhere in the lower regions turned my stomach, and I experienced none of the joys of the cruel sea. I was in fact horribly ill for almost the entire journey, although I was just able to emerge at the end of it to enjoy the unbelievable beauties of Rio, with its mountains behind, the gigantic blue butterflies, the blue and white foam of the enormous breakers on its honey-coloured sands, and the majestic Copacabana. As a contrast to this, the murky San Paulo that I had seen on the way there,

[1] A cattle-farm in Spanish America.

with its sunken hulks, which for centuries had lain there
as reminders of the terrible plague that had stricken it and
which had made it necessary in the distant past to scuttle
its ships and burn its homes. Most of the passengers had
gone ashore there to see a snake farm some two hours'
journey away, but for me the sunken ships still held evil
and, as I hate snakes anyway, I had seen no point in join-
ing the expedition. We had now reached the River Plate,
whose muddy waters need perpetual dredging to keep the
channel deep enough for its shipping. There is something
exciting in its ugliness, as if it were warning one to turn
back now before it is too late, but soon the giant sky-
scrapers came into view, and here we were at last in the
country of my hopes and dreams. I had bought two
canaries when we had stopped at Madeira, for I had felt
they would be companions to me in the vast loneliness I
was heading for; but then I knew nothing about a law
which forbids one to bring more than one canary into the
country – a law, I gather, intended to protect the country
in some way from getting over-run with breeding canaries,
though I fail to see what harm would come of it. The
customs man was adamant that only one must come in;
but still I begged and pleaded and finally they sent for an
official from the Ministry of Agriculture who, armed with
sheaves of documents, tried to work the problem out from
every angle, and at last, helped by a quietly slipped-in tip,
decided that, as I was destined for the very far north where
the canaries would probably die in any case, they both
should be allowed to come in. I felt quite exhausted after
this set-to, and was glad to see my host on the quay and
to leave to him the task of clearing my luggage through
the customs.

Our train for the *estancia* was due to leave at two o'clock,
so we had just sufficient time to return to the hotel for
lunch and for a quick bath. When I came to pay, I found
I was short of money, and of course the banks were not
open on Sunday, so I asked at the hotel desk if they would

change a cheque for me on an English bank, which without hesitation they said they would. This surprised me greatly, for I was a complete stranger there and they neither asked me for a reference nor asked me to tell them where I was going to afterwards. How times have changed!

Two o'clock came and the train left on our eight-hundred-mile journey up country. Everyone had a sleeper for what it was worth, but the sanitary arrangements on the train were too dreadful, and I was warned not to attempt to wash in the basin, for fear that it might have been used for other purposes.

We travelled much of the way in the dining-car, as one could see out from it on all sides, and naturally I was anxious to miss nothing. For miles and miles the scenery changed little, small houses with *patios*, surrounded by orange trees, all the houses in the little streets being flat-faced and white-washed, with tropical creepers growing up the *patio* supports. Everywhere people seemed to be resting, and I was told it was the siesta time, when the whole country stops for three hours – shops close, work stops and silence reigns supreme. I found this habit most annoying all the time I was out there, for I myself never developed the desire to sleep during the day, and on those occasions when I had to ride sixty miles to the little town to do my shopping, I thought it a wicked waste of time and money to have to book a room to retire to in the local hotel when all I wanted to do was to ride home as soon as my shopping was done, which in the circumstances I found it difficult to do before curfew.

After two hours in the train we came to a ferry, where we were kept waiting for ages. The train had to be driven onto the ferry-boat for a five-hour journey upstream, but the army were on manoeuvres and had taken away the ferry unexpectedly – just like that! It didn't seem to matter to them at all that the passengers were inconvenienced, or that the railway officials in Buenos Aires had not been notified of what had taken place, and I was to learn that this sort of thing happened continually. However, we set off eventually and were able at last to stretch our legs walking about on the ferry. The river was murky with great reeds growing on either side, and beyond it was flat and uninviting. Small native reed-thatched houses were scattered about, and in the distance we saw a few miserable cattle and poultry. I soon retired and slept quite well, only to be woken in the morning by the rattle of shunting as we were now once more on rails on dry land. I went to the dining-car as soon as I could to see if there was any breakfast going, and there I got coffee and rolls, but in the meantime I was being eaten alive by flies. I had had no experience before, except for horseflies, of flies attacking human beings, but this variety certainly did, and we spent most of our time swatting them and trying to evade them.

The country had now changed: one no longer saw houses and orange groves, but pampas for as far as the eye could see, and just a single telegraph wire that ran along by the railway line. From time to time we passed little farmstead homes of mud and thatch, each with a Hornero, or oven bird, nesting on its gate in its own little round house. I discovered later that these birds build their round-shaped mud nests with a corner to go round inside, in order to protect their eggs and their young from their natural foes, the only enemy that could possibly get round the bend being a snake. It was for this reason that I was warned never to put my hand inside one of these nests for fear that a snake might already have taken a lease of it for its home.

My eyes were kept glued to the window on the look-out for beautiful horses, but I saw very few young ones, only a few elderly animals tied up to poles near the houses, with heads drooping, and resting their weary legs one at a time. Suddenly the air began to darken and a most horrible smell filtered up through the floorboards of the train; the engine seemed to be working harder than usual, yet we were making little progress. The explanation was – locusts! Millions of them had descended on the area and they were being run over by the train. This was causing the railway lines to get slippery, and although the gradient was only a slight one the train was now skidding hopelessly. The sun was already blacked out and the swirling masses of brown creatures were hitting themselves against the windows. A few of them got in – great grasshoppers they seemed – and one of them came and sat quite happily on my hand. The train by now was at a standstill and the attendant told us that we should have to stay there either until another engine came to help us or until the locusts moved on: this they would do when everything edible had been devoured, which clearly wouldn't take very long. We watched the inhabitants of a mud hut running around madly, banging tins and saucepans to try and save their little plots of gardens, but within half an hour every tree in sight was bare of all leaves, and the whole place looked as if it had had a plague, as indeed it had. The locusts went as suddenly as they had come, and slowly the train started on its way again, carrying with it for some time the dreadful smell of burning locusts. After seemingly endless hours of the same monotonous countryside and evil smells, we finally arrived at our station, there to find our hosts, an English couple, with whom we were to stay for that night; they had an *estancia* near the station. The hour was too late for us to complete the long journey by the rough roads that still had to be traversed before I reached my new home.

The *estancia* where this middle-aged couple lived belonged to the same Company that owned the one I was going to myself, but it was a far superior one, the manager being an area supervisor and his *estancia* being used for the directors to stay in when they came out on official business and inspections. In fact it possessed all that one could need for comfort, with bathrooms, electric light, telephone and so on; also lovely buildings which housed magnificent thoroughbred stallions, and a vast number of beautiful brood mares, that had been crossed with thoroughbreds to improve the native strain of pony. Here were no creolla cattle, but pedigree Herefords instead, that were destined for the *frigoríficos*[2] and the frozen-meat market – the lean creolla cattle were bred for beef products and the tinned meat market. Incidentally they couldn't have used the glorious fat Herefords for the canning trade, because the fat would have caused the tins to blow. I learnt this on my first visit to the factory, where I followed a batch of our cattle right through the process from *estancia* to shop. We all spent a most pleasant and instructive day with these kind people, and in the evening the men took guns and the manager's wife and I followed them across the camp, as the land surrounding an *estancia* is always called. With us came an old pointer bitch and her seven ten-week-old puppies, which fascinated me by showing their hunting skill at that tender age. Mother pointer flushed a partridge and stood immobile with quivering tail outstretched; and then all the puppies made a circle round and pointed also, keeping quite still except for their typically quivering tails. How I wished that I had a camera with me, for it would have been a snap in a million! What the partridge thought, when it eventually rose from this sea of dogs, I don't know, but it was allowed its freedom.

Next morning we started on the last part of our trek to the *estancia*, a wonderful old 'Tin Lizzie' being our conveyance. The Argentine driver seemed in an almighty hurry, and took bumps at such speed I was often nearly shot out. Once, we were going particularly fast along a straight but bumpy road, when a partridge suddenly got up and, in a fraction of a second, with one hand still adhering to the wheel, the man whipped out his revolver and shot the bird. He laughed, stopped the car, picked the partridge up, and then with an exaggerated bow handed it over to me. I felt that, whatever happened after that, I would never get on the wrong side of him or of anyone like him!

Some hours later, and without anything worse than a stiff neck and aching bones, we arrived at the *estancia*

[2] Freezing or cold store.

which was to be my home for some time to come. It was
set in a lovely grove of eucalyptus trees; a windmill idled
away nearby and, except for a large barn, no other buildings were visible anywhere, just pampas for as far as the
eye could see. The house was long and low, with its inevitable *patio*. Some scruffy chickens, and some Muscovy ducks
with the typical red blobs over their noses, were the only
livestock in sight. I was told that the horses were all
turned out some miles away in the camp, and that the
peons[3] (the equivalent of cowboys) were away counting
the sheep and cattle of the *estancia*.

A wrinkled old Argentino came up and bid us good day,
and helped us in with the luggage, and the old cook and
her satin-skinned fifteen-year-old daughter came out to greet
us, before we sat down to our meal of hard rolls and
dripping or jam. Butter there was unprocurable, the only
people who ever made it being the Jewish settlers, who
were the most industrious workers in the neighbourhood. It
was impossible for us on our *estancia* to make butter
because it was against the rules of the company even to
keep a single special house-cow, for it was ordained that all
cows should be suckling calves. When we needed milk in
the house, old Fernandez would go out on his horse to
round up some likely-looking young matrons, and bring
them into the corral with their calves; he would then lasso
them one at a time and extract as much milk as possible
from each unwilling cow. It was a risky business getting
it from a wild and kicking cow, and sometimes it took
eight or more cows to produce the half-gallon we needed.
It seemed to me a most fantastically stupid rule, but out
there Company's rules were rules, and no one dared break
them.

It was due to this stupid rule, as it happened, that I
myself caught foot-and-mouth disease; for one of the cows
that had been rounded up must have been suffering from it,
and a human being can easily catch the disease after drink-

[3] *Peons*=farm-workers.

ing milk from an infected cow. That is one of the reasons for the slaughter policy in Great Britain; but out there nobody bothers much about foot-and-mouth disease. Of course the cattle get it, and become terribly thin, but eventually they get over it and are then said to be the ones that fatten best. Very occasionally an animal cannot stand the fortnight or so of starvation and dies; but that is the exception rather than the rule. When I had it myself, I suffered greatly. In the human being the disease affects only the mouth, but great ulcers form on the inside of the cheek and soft palate, one's saliva runs just like a tap, and one cannot eat anything, but only take small sips of broth. I had to have a large rough towel tied under my chin, which got completely soaked in no time and had often to be changed, and I had to sleep as best as I could sitting up, or I should have choked with the persistently running saliva. Everyone kept away from me for a time, for fear of carrying the disease to the foreman's little children who lived in a small hut nearby, for, if their new baby had caught it, it would almost certainly have died. I recovered completely in about a fortnight, and was very much thinner but otherwise quite unharmed. I can never catch it again, thank goodness!

After tea on that first day at my new home, I walked round the house and discovered what a dreadful place it was, without curtains and with only rickety old iron bedsteads, with no fireplace in the sitting-room, and a completely Heath-Robinson bath. The latter consisted of an ordinary bath indoors, connected with a pipe attached to a sort of copper outside. Whenever one wanted a bath, old Fernandez was asked to fill the copper with water from the windmill; this, even using two buckets, took a considerable time to do, including all the walking to and fro. Then a fire was lit underneath the copper and so the water from the bath got heated. It gave only just sufficient for one rather meagre bath, and old Fernandez simply hated the job of filling the copper, nothing putting him in a worse temper, especially as he saw no reason for what seemed to him this fastidious behaviour. In the hot season, of course, we used simply to ride out to the large windmill tanks that were situated all over the camp and have a swim in them. They were four or five feet deep and about eight yards across, so one could have quite a nice cooling swim. The cattle didn't much approve of our swimming in their drinking water, and used to stand with sad, disillusioned eyes staring at us, and not daring to come very near.

Sometimes, in the drought, the cattle got too weak to reach the windmills, being so starved from lack of grass, and they would die in their hundreds from thirst. It was one of the saddest sights imaginable to see hundreds of sheep lambing down in a drought and having no milk at all to give to their lambs. It used to drive me nearly mad with rage not to be able to get milk from the cows to rear those lambs with; but my old cook and I did what we could, and we regularly had about twenty-five orphans around the house. But tragedy would come to us again when they grew up and had to go down in the company's counting of stock, eventually to be slaughtered. I think most people who love animals as I do suffer continually, for one's animals grow old so soon, or have to be killed like my lambs. I wish one could get hardened to it, but I never do.

Soon after my arrival at the *estancia*, I went to look at the horses, and was given a little roan pony to ride. I revelled in his beautiful smooth action, all the ponies out there being taught the effortless canter on a loose rein, which makes it possible for one to travel long distances without fatigue. Their other pace is a very slow amble; by the use of long stirrups and neck-reining the horse, one does not rise to the trot, and this seems to be the perfect method of riding. I can never understand how English people can enjoy riding on their horses' mouths, with short stirrups and no neck-reining. But then, I have always ridden by giving signals to my horse with my voice and my legs, and by neck-reining for guidance.

The number of horses on that camp simply staggered me. There were over two thousand brood mares with their foals, and in addition there were the yearlings, the three-year-olds, and the *tropillos*[4] or troops of working horses for the employees. Each *peon* or cowboy had twelve horses of a certain colour to use for the month that they were at work. At the end of the month those horses were pretty near skeletons and were turned free, and another *tropilla* was caught up. The *peons* were all responsible for their own horses and changed them about as became necessary. The foreman, or *capitas*[5] as he was called, had the most beautiful horses of the lot. He was an expert at working in plaited rawhide and in Paraguayan silver, and on his *fiesta*[6] days, when he rode to town, he looked magnificent, silver on his spurs and on his bridle, and reins dotted with silver, and under his *ricardo*[7] or saddle his horse carried a lovely patterned wool cloth made by his wife. I got her to make me one of these lovely blankets for my own saddle, for, although I always rode with an English saddle, it was extremely comfortable for the horse, and a good protection for my saddle also to have a thick blanket underneath it. No horse ever got a sore back with one of these. They were made of unwashed sheep's wool, with all the natural oils left in, the colours coming from herbal dyes.

When I first went out, I was given three horses to use, and one was always kept saddled up and tied to our front *patio*, so that if I wanted to go out I only had to step into the saddle. But it annoyed me to be treated as rather an inferior being and not to be allowed to ride out into the camp with the men to see what was going on – but women were indeed inferior creatures out there. I plaited the manes of my three mounts, and pulled and bandaged their tails and groomed them all until they shone – but that didn't take up the whole day! So I would ride out into the camp to keep myself occupied; but it was boring riding broken

---

[4] *Tropilla*=troop or group.   [5] *Capitas*=foreman.
[6] *Fiesta*=holiday or feast day   [7] *Ricardo*=saddle outfit.

animals. Soon I got a jump put up, and began teaching them to jump, and to play polo, and it wasn't long before these three knew almost everything.

My life out there at first was extremely tedious. The day started for the men in summer at about three a.m., for it was cool then for working the cattle. But I never got up at that time, as I shouldn't have had anything to do. I used to get up at about five-thirty, and take one of my ponies out for a ride, for that is the most beautiful time for riding out there. Everything smells sweet and fresh before the great heat drives one to darkened rooms and mosquito nets and the smell of anti-fly sprays. The flowers open early to greet the morning sun; and the colour of the verbenas, which grow in wild profusion on the camp, has to be seen rather than described for the full glory of nature's paintbox to be appreciated. I used to return to breakfast alone; the folk from the *estancia* had eaten a stew or roast before they left and would not now be back until midday at the earliest, according to where they were working. I had no work to do because English women don't do work on an *estancia* unless they wish to cook; household help is cheap, and I was told at the very beginning that if I wanted even the matches off the mantelpiece I should call Maria to get them for me. She appeared to love to do things like this, and never seemed to object to being called for the most trivial things. I can't say I myself called her much, but the Boss certainly did.

When I wasn't riding, or feeding my *guacha*[8] lambs, or cleaning my saddle, I was left to do the only things I could do, knit or write long letters home. It was while I was sitting on the *patio* writing home one day that I heard what I thought was a motor-cycle approaching, a racing motor-cycle at that, the noise being that of one without a silencer. The dog jumped up and barked furiously; I stood up and anxiously scanned the horizon, terribly excited at the thought of seeing a fresh face. But it wasn't until the

[8] *Guacha*=orphan.

noise sounded quite close to my ear that I realized it was coming from the wings of a tiny little green and blue humming bird, collecting the nectar of a flower growing up the *patio*. His wings were beating the air at such a rate that this fantastic noise was created. He was hovering, stationary in the air, with his beak in the flower head. I caught him and he didn't seem at all frightened; he was so tiny that his whole length was no greater than the distance from my thumb nail to my first thumb joint. I freed him and he again set up this loud noise as he set about his work unconcernedly. That is the first and only time I saw anything resembling him out there, and the next time I saw his species was in the Brighton Museum.

I used to ride again in the evening when the heat of the day was over. Life always stands still in the Argentine from eleven o'clock until two, or twelve until three, according to the season and sun. The heat is too great to do any work, and people who live out there soon get the midday sleep habit.

When the men came home at night, the evening meal was served, either outdoors in the shade of the tangerine tree or in the cool of a darkened room. All shutters are closed during the heat of the day so that the rooms may be bearably cool in the evening. We used to play cards most evenings, and I learnt to be most cunning over poker, though I refused to play for money. Usually I got left out of it as being a spoilsport. Bridge was the game we all liked to play most, but there were few chances unless English people came to stay, a rare and very welcome treat. Then we played all day and all night; tempers got frayed, mine not least, as I used to indulge in psychic bidding. I had beginner's luck, and seldom lost, although I should have done so according to the rules. I fear I never really liked cards, and the seriousness with which these games were played seemed silly to me. But I suppose when one has as little fun as that kind of life offered, these games became important.

I think I have shown how unvaried and purposeless life was until the time came when I was allowed to break horses for a living. To be happy while doing little beyond idling my days away was not easy for me, but once I had the horses to break it was a totally different matter.

It was now that I started pressing to be allowed to break in some of the horses myself, because for over a year past I had had to satisfy myself with giving already tamed horses their extra schooling. That began to bore me, so I decided to learn to be a cook in my spare time. I had English magazines sent out to me by my mother, and in the weekly *Home Chat* I found enclosed a free gift of a cookery pamphlet having the interesting title of 'Goodies for the Party'; so instead of starting at 'how to boil an egg', I began at the other end with meringues and macaroons and walnut layer cakes, etc. I ordered a large box of provisions from Harrods at Buenos Aires, with such items as nuts, and rice paper, and glacé cherries, and much to the amusement of our old Indian cook, I set out to prepare dishes which neither she nor I had ever made before or even knew how to make. At first I found great difficulty in regulating the oven, since we had only a wood-burning range, and the heat of your oven depended on how much wood and draught you had.

After my first visit to the shops to get some fancy baking tins, I was quite excited at the thought of starting my very experimental cookery. 'Beginner's luck', again, and beginner's luck my cookery certainly had. Everything we made from the little pamphlet seemed to turn out right, and thank goodness it did, because it was not long after our experiments began that, without any warning whatsoever, the English directors turned up to lunch and tea. Lunch is easy enough : a sheep or a lamb is killed, and an *asado* or roast is done on a spit outside. Everyone sits down with a knife and eats his fill off the knife, and there is little ceremony.

But I had different ideas. I knew that things had not been going too well lately on the *estancia*, a severe drought having caused serious losses in sheep and cattle, and the *estancia* was not paying its way as it should. I thought that if I could produce a tasty lunch it might mellow the bosses a bit. Fernandez had already been persuaded to make a vegetable garden behind the house and he had been quite successful in growing beans, and peas, and melons, so we decided on lamb chops 'à la Milanese', which consisted of dipping the chops in vinegar and then egg-and-bread-crumbing them and frying them lightly. In addition we had potato chips and young broad beans. Then there were meringues, filled with vanilla cornflour mixture as we had no cream, and the meal was finished off with a tiny melon for each guest, with coffee to follow. It would have served them right if they'd had to drink it black, with the silly regulations that they made about not having a house-cow! I kept them talking as long as I dared, and flirted outrageously with a rather susceptible Argentine Inspector who accompanied them, for I knew it was his knowledge, mostly, that was the be-all and sometimes the end-all of these jobs. Apparently everything went off as well as could be expected, and old Maria and I felt we had done our bit.

On my rare visits to town I had to have the faithful help and companionship of old Fernandez; we each drove twelve horses ahead of us and covered the whole distance at a slow canter. At every five miles or so approximately we would stop if we saw a *puesta*[9] and ask permission to turn a horse out until our return. This meant of course that every new horse we used did a distance of five miles further than the previous one, although we never actually rode one horse for more than five miles. This last one to be ridden actually had to cover the full sixty miles, and for this last hop I usually kept my favourite grey Arab mare, who was so smooth to ride that I could actually go to sleep on her as I rode. They all followed the bell mare in front until the last changeover, when the bell mare herself was ridden by Fernandez. Whenever I felt that I needed a little sleep, I

[9] Small outpost.

used just to set my mare near Fernandez and she would keep up her steady pace alongside him, never faltering – I believe that our understanding was so great that she would have kept me on her back whichever way I leaned. When we arrived in the town Fernandez took the horses to one of the local tie-ups for water, and we arranged to meet again at a fixed time and place. I was now left alone to do whatever I wished. Usually we rode back at nightfall, by the light of the moon, as it was cooler then both for ourselves and for the horses. It took about eight hours' riding to get there, having started at about three o'clock in the morning. This time, when I set off for town, I was asked by the manager to buy him a pair of pyjamas, and I thought that an easy task as the word is the same in Spanish as it is in English. I got on very well with buying the things I needed myself, and then went to a men's outfitters and general stores and asked for *pyjamas*. The assistant understood what I wanted and brought out some boxes. I chose a simple pattern, left the shop, and thought no more of the matter until I returned to the *estancia*. The manager then opened the parcel and held up the jacket, and to my horror I saw that that was all there was in the box. The explanation was that the pyjama jacket out there was the Sunday-go-to-meeting wear of the smart Argentino. He wears black trousers, or if he hasn't these, baggy *bombachos*[10] (which are like plus-fours but in cotton) tucked into his soft leather riding boots, a pyjama jacket, a scarf, and a felt hat, and no one in the camp ever dreams of wearing pyjamas for night attire. Did I feel a fool!

The time to see all this smart garb is on a Saturday evening, in the Plaza of the little town. All towns have their Plazas, and on these occasions the young men of the district doll themselves up in their very best and parade round and round. The señoritas do the same, but they walk round in the opposite direction, always in twos and threes, and it is in this preliminary inspection that the young men decide

[10] *Bombachos*=native trousers.

whom to ask to be their partners in the dancing that follows. In every small town national lottery tickets are for sale for enormous prizes, and there are very few people who do not take at least one ticket; these are usually for sale on the same day as the dancing takes place, for it is then that outsiders from cattle and sheep *estancias* come into the town with money to spend. I used to stay to watch the young peacocks strutting round and to see the dancing that followed – but not for long, for there was always that journey home to keep in mind.

It was not long after this that we had a terrific freak storm and whirlwind. I had never seen or heard anything like it in my life. Roofs just went up into the sky, and sheep into eucalyptus trees. It also caused a most unhealthy state of affairs with regard to a child's coffin that had been suspended high up in a eucalyptus tree, where the natives put children's coffins, believing that a child when it dies must not be buried under the ground where the angels cannot reach it. So they make a little white coffin, and the poor little corpse is battened down inside and hung up in a tree. This particular storm brought one of these pathetic little coffins hurtling to the ground, and the bones were spread around, which was considered a very bad omen indeed. There was much crossing of themselves the next day, when as reverently as they could they collected the remains together again and replaced them in the little coffin, which again they firmly fixed on high.

This terrific storm caused many unusual phenomena. All night the wind howled and the rain came down as in a cloudburst. But at dawn it stopped as suddenly as it had begun, and we all went out to see what damage had been done. The first thing we saw was a river racing over the gulleys where formerly there had been no river. And now we saw fish, great big fish, where there had been none before, the nearest river being thirty miles away at least. I can only suppose that the whirlwind had picked them up and dropped them for us, like the miracle of the fishes –

that at any rate is how most people would prefer to explain it. We hadn't seen fish since we left England and it was the greatest possible treat to eat them now. I weighed the one I took in and found it to be six pounds exactly. We baked it, after consulting my cookery book, and served it with tartare sauce! And very tasty it was too.

Shortly after the storm, the foreman's little son came rushing up to say that all his pet rabbits had gone and that in the cage instead was a baby skunk. The mother had perished in the storm and lay dead by the cage. How that living little skunk got into the undamaged cage, and the rabbits out of it, was beyond our understanding. In the mother's pouch were two dead babies. Experts cannot account for a skunk with a pouch, and try to persuade me that she was a 'possum. But she was no 'possum: she had the bushy tail of a skunk and was identical with the skunk picture in Cassell's *Book of Knowledge*. She did have a pouch: I examined her closely.

Anyway, I took the wee mite from the boy and put it on an old jumper in the oven, which was now only warm. I then heated some milk, and with my fountain-pen filler got a few drops into its mouth. In quite a short time it seemed quite perky again, and I decided that, as it was a pouch-living baby, it must have something of the same sort now, so I popped it into the pocket of the riding skirt I was wearing. I lined the pocket with cotton wool, in case of accidents, and for a whole week my baby thrived there. He remained in my pocket when I went riding, and I wondered how he liked the motion. At night I wrapped him up warmly with a hot bottle for company. But, alas, he escaped from his wrapping one night and got severely chilled, and all my loving care was of no avail in saving his life. I am afraid I wept unashamedly when I found him dead. He had seemed such a sweet little thing, holding on to the pen filler with his little paws, that looked so much like hands, and sucking contentedly.

Talking of skunks, I learnt from my old cook that if

one gets up and rides out into the camp at sunrise, one will see the meeting of the skunks. I rode out to see this one morning early and sure enough I saw a fascinating sight, about twelve of them sitting in a horseshoe, with one old chap at the head, just as we used to sit round the Brown Owl when we were Brownies as children. The old skunk at the top seemed to be briefing his family in the work of the day. They paid no attention to me. I watched them for about fifteen minutes, when suddenly they all got up and ran down their holes. One day one of the *estancia* dogs got too near one and came home exuding a terrible smell. My baby skunk had been too young to have a smell.

The storm was followed by another calamity in the form of smallpox. An outbreak occurred some distance away and the unprepared natives died like flies. We ourselves got orders at once from the Company to vaccinate all our employees. They sent us lymph from Buenos Aires, but no instruments to do it with; so I sterilized the scalpel in my manicure set, thinking that that would just about do the trick, if Fernandez sharpened it for me, and one by one I gave them a scratch and smeared it with lymph. Some days later a furious *peon* arrived on my doorstep demanding another scratch; he had had no reaction, and his pals had told him it was because he was not a strong and virile man. So I did it again for him, assuring him that it was just because he *was* a big strong man, while his friends were weak and susceptible, that it had not come up, and that that showed he was not very liable to catch the disease. And that quite satisfied him.

It was extraordinary the amount of medical work that came my way, considering that my only knowledge of it came from the three years I had spent at an agricultural college, where the curriculum had included a short course of veterinary science. But the people had great faith in an Englishwoman's knowledge of ills of all kinds, although they have a local *curandera*[11] of their own, whom they call

11 *Curandera*=healer.

in when their women are in childbirth, and she was supposed by all to have a great knowledge of herbal cures. I don't know what English doctors would think of the native Argentine ways when their offspring are brought into the world, but they certainly wouldn't conform to our standards here. The old *curandera*, heavily robed in black from head to toe, comes and takes up residence with the expectant mother about a fortnight before the baby is due to arrive, and when the birth is imminent all the windows and doors are heavily boarded up and the house is made completely dark, except for one candle. Both the husband and the *curandera* support the labouring mother when her time arrives. After the birth the baby is not washed, but is just wrapped up as it was born, until the third day, when the shutters are taken down again. The baby is then washed at last, and the mother once more goes about her daily tasks. The old *curandera* stays about a month altogether and is treated extremely well during her visit, as a sort of insurance against future ills. I often wondered whether she herself ever washed or took off her black garments.

I referred above to the woman's 'husband' helping during labour; but in the true sense of the word he is not her husband, as they have not gone through any marriage ceremony. The natives, where I used to live, choose their *companieras* (wives) from a local family, and the taking of the girl home to their *puesta* constitutes in their eyes a binding contract, to which they remain faithful all their lives. I never heard of any man leaving his 'wife', or vice versa, and they bring up their children together, just as if they were in fact married; for in their eyes and in the eyes of the world the children of such a 'marriage' are just as legitimate as if their parents were married in a legal manner. They have many children, who from an early age learn to ride horses bareback, and are accustomed to helping their father or to running messages for their mother and to do other small tasks. They all live together in the one- or two-roomed native hut with no division of the sexes at all. Even the old *curandera* joins in without worrying about the close quarters or about segregation.

When anyone is ill, they make a wonderful mixture of milk and sugar called *dulce de leche*, which is supposed to be so concentrated in its efficacy that the weakest patient can live on a very small amount. I was constantly offered this food by the foreman's wife when I had diabetes, for she thought it would do me good, but it would of course in fact have done me much harm owing to its high sugar content. Its taste is rather like that of fudge and honey mixed and its consistency is similar to that of honey.

The small children of the natives spend hours of their lives perched on orange-boxes on the *patio*, where they are put to sit by their mothers, who know that they cannot get down and thus get into mischief while she is busy doing her chores. I have often seen the foreman's two-year-old son perched on his orange-box for three or four hours at a time, with nothing to play with and quite silent – yet he was a bright and intelligent little lad. At the age of four he used to go off galloping into the camp on a small fat cowpony. The little girls had blankets on the backs of their ponies, which were kept in place by a surcingle; they sat sideways on their ponies, but succeeded in galloping about quite happily. How on earth they stayed on I simply don't know. Very often an old Granny and a child would ride on the same pony together in this fashion. I never saw a native woman riding astride in the Argentine, for even if they have a *ricardo* they ride on it side-saddle and without a pommel.

It is amazing to me how contented with their lot they all seemed – a visit to the little village once a month appeared to be all that they wanted. Their rations of farina and meat came from the *estancia*, and were handed out to all the employees weekly. Most of them kept little gardens, where they grew sweet potatoes, and they all had chickens, for which they grew maize, and many of them kept Muscovy ducks and turkeys as well. They all dried wafer-thin slices of meat on lines in the sun, just like hanging out the washing. The meat dried in the hot sun until it was almost like leather, and was then packed away in boxes with salt. When they wanted meat, and no fresh meat was being killed, it was taken out and soaked for a few hours before cooking, and it was certainly delicious. To me at first it seemed so wrong that the meat should be exposed to the dust and flies in this way, but, after I had tasted it, I decided that it was tender and quite delicious – and after all it was well boiled before use, being always eaten in a stew. Into the stew went sweet potatoes, *choclos* or maize cobs, macaroni, and farina, the ground flour. The oldest member of the family did practically nothing else but sit with a long-handled spoon stirring the stew, which seemed always to be on the hob. The lack of green vegetables was counteracted by the drinking of the herbal maté tea, and they never otherwise saw green vegetables at all. We English people grew them, but the natives never seemed to bother.

I think the faith that the natives had in their *curanderas* was fading fast when I was there, for I found that the people so often came to me with their troubles, which I treated as best I could with the homoeopathic remedies that my mother had brought us up with. I remember one day one of the outpost men came riding in to me in a great hurry, saying that his baby was dying and asking for my help. So I got onto my horse, and sure enough the child had a temperature of over a hundred and five, and, as I thought, had meningitis. I knew that I must get a doctor to it really quickly if it was not to be too late, so I set off once more with Fernandez on the fifteen-mile ride to the doctor who lived nearest to us, who although unqualified was said to be very clever. But I had been told that he wouldn't come out except for me or the manager, and he seldom would. However, I arrived at his door and he answered my knock. He said that he would come for sixty pesos, then worth about three pounds, but that he wouldn't even put on his hat if I didn't pay him in advance. This put me in a quandary for I had no money with me and Fernandez had only a few pesos. So I begged and begged him to come, and promised payment just as soon as the *patrón* got back. But no, he would not come. So in desperation I went off to a Jewish smallholder with whom I had talked horses once or twice, and he generously lent me the money straightaway. We all rode back as fast as our horses would carry us, and the doctor when he got there did a lumbar puncture that saved the child's life.

I often had to deal with terrible wounds in the horses. They would get kicked by another one, or gored by steers, or sometimes torn terribly on the barbed wire. I used to stitch them up as best I could with an ordinary darning needle and boiled thread. I found that some got well quite easily with antiseptic treatment, but others would go septic. It was then that I learnt from the natives to allow the flies to blow the wound; for then, when the grubs hatched out, they consumed all the diseased and foul matter. At first this sounded to me simply too dreadful, but I tried it out in desperation with a horse whose skin on its face had been torn away and was flapping over its nose, after it had caught its head between corral bars. I had stitched it back into place in the way I practised at first, but it had gone septic, so I opened up a stitch or two and in the hot sun the flies obligingly laid their eggs amidst the wound's smelliness. After some days the grubs hatched out and ate the wound clean, as the natives had said they would, and I was able to close it up again, beautifully pink and clean, after washing all the grubs out with disinfectant, and the wound healed quickly and almost without a scar.

Quite one of the most frightening experiences I had was once when I was alone on the *estancia*. Fernandez was taking the big stallion out to drink, as it was always shut up in the barn, normally, in the foaling season. Suddenly it bucked; he dropped its rope and it bucked again, kicking him full on the head. He dropped like a stone, and I saw that his skull was fractured at one side. I ran to the house for my cook as fast as I could, and together we carried him in to bed. I then pushed the protruding pieces firmly back together again and applied a pad of homoeopathic tincture of Calendula[12], which was all that I had. We didn't expect the men back for days, so I couldn't go for a doctor, for I knew that it was never safe to go off the camp alone. About twenty-four hours later he recovered consciousness, and I continued to nurse him for about three weeks, when he became well enough to go by borrowed car to hospital, where they X-rayed him and did a lumbar puncture. They soon reported him perfectly all right again, and I thanked God for his stamina and for the success of my humble efforts.

[12] African marigold.

4 Horse-breaking
without Fears

To anyone who has not been to South America, to one of the bigger cattle *estancias* out there, it may sound fantastic that anyone should have a holding covering a hundred square miles, that took a week to ride round. The one I was on had sixty thousand head of beef cattle that had been trekked from the north to the fattening grass of our *estancias*. These were creolla cattle, long horned and thin, but with terrific stamina. Most of them had been half-starved all their lives, and had to be acclimatized to the lusher pastures further south. They also had to learn not to eat the poisonous 'Mio Mio' plant, which did not grow in the place they had come from and to which they were not accustomed. To teach them, they were put in a corral and a great quantity of the plant was burnt round them all night. The smell of the smoke so created seemed to give them a hatred of the plant itself, and they were then safe to be turned loose in the camp. Cattle that have been reared on an *estancia* where the plant grows do not need this immunization, but graze happily amongst it and never touch it.

A curious sight for the newcomer to the pampas is the way the natural roads are always in waves, absolutely parallel and regular. This is so because the cattle that are being trekked south always step exactly in each other's footsteps. The mud bakes in the sun and the roads stay like that for ever. They become quite impassable for other traffic, so any motors have to pioneer their own road nearby. These roads can be extremely dangerous, for directly the rain comes they turn into a morass in a matter of minutes, and if you are driving a car you can be up to your axles and completely stuck in a very short time. I well remember getting caught like this when, after many years of having to ride sixty miles or so to do my shopping, we invested in an old Buick. In great excitement we set off to meet some English neighbours in a town about a hundred miles away. The weather looked perfect and the natives gave us no warning of impending storms. But perhaps this was deliberate, for they saw nothing but evil in the car we had bought. Anyway, at about six o'clock in the evening, I felt a queer premonition that it was going to rain and, in spite of the fact that the sky looked clear and everyone laughed me to scorn, I insisted that the menfolk from the *estancia* should leave their drinking and start for home. Many rude remarks were made about what a nuisance women were, but I ignored them all, for I was becoming intensely nervous, foreseeing danger. We hadn't gone more than twenty miles on the way back when I was proved to be right; the sky darkened, and soon the night became full of the most glorious coloured lightning imaginable – mauve, red, yellow, blue, and green – distant thunder boomed and growled, and enormous spots of rain spattered our windscreen. We were miles from anywhere, with open pampas for as far as the eye could see, without even a native mud hut. I myself was driving, and I put my foot down as hard as I dared. The nearest village was San Salvador, some ten leagues away, but I knew we had no hope of reaching there, for the roads even then, with the spotting rain, were becoming greasy. The clouds raced up, the thunder roared, and at once down in a cloudburst came the rain. I skidded furiously, trembling with fear; the car became unmanageable and slid to a stop with its nose over a nasty drop. We got out, to find the mud already up to the axle, and we soon realized that without horses to pull us out we should be marooned there indefinitely. We had no food, and we were shivering with cold. It is amazing how cold it becomes when it rains like that. The thirsty ground can clearly be heard ticking quite loudly as it drinks and expands. Two hours passed, and I said rather nasty things about not listening to a woman's intuition. The men were ominously silent, worried as to our future as the car sank lower and lower in the mud. Just as we were wondering whether one of the party should set off to see if a native hut could anywhere be found, three men rode up on horseback. We told them of our plight and offered a large reward if they could tow us with their horses to any sort of safety. Luckily for us they said that about a league down the road was a little *puesta* where we could shelter. The three horses had their lassos tied on to the car and tried their best to pull it out, but it would not budge. So the men left, and an hour later came back with eleven horses in all, with the help of which we were towed to shelter.

If one has never seen the squalor of an Argentine *puesta*, one cannot imagine what it means to an English person to stay there. The walls of the houses are made of biscuit tins opened out and nailed to a frame of wood; then when the rains come and the mud is soft the owners plaster the biscuit-tin walls with mud. The great heat from the sun bakes it hard and so the house is made. There is no chimney, but only a hole in the roof, nor any windows. The average number of people living in a ten-by-ten house is about eight, without counting the innumerable chickens and *guacha* lambs (orphans). It is the custom of the Argentinos to take innumerable sips of maté tea throughout the day. This is made in a gourd, with a silver *bombilla*[1] or pipe to drink from, and every visitor, out of courtesy, must take his sip in turn. As the gourd is passed round, boiling water from the smoky fire is added after every sip, which I think saves the spread of disease, for I cannot imagine a more certain disseminator of germs than this ghastly habit. Here then was I, faced with taking sips of

[1] *Bombilla*=a thin pipe like a drinking-straw made of Paraguayan silver.

this hateful stuff or offending our hosts. But, luckily, when it was handed to me one of my friends saved the situation by saying that I had only just come from England, where we did not drink maté, and would they excuse me.

It was already late, so we dossed down in indescribable filth and stench for one of the worst nights I have spent in the whole of my life. Darkness is an invitation in itself to all the millions of *bichos*,[2] which include mosquitoes, beetles of every known variety, and all the other creeping things, and I was 'the target for tonight'! Perhaps I was not as immune as my tougher friends who had lived out there for many years, and there certainly wasn't an inch of me that hadn't been sucked or tickled by these bugs when dawn came and the making of the fire drove the creepy-crawlies of the night to retire and digest their spoils.

As dawn broke the rain stopped, brilliant sun came out, and I saw a sight that I shall remember to my dying day. The pampas had turned pink for as far as the eye could see, with millions and millions of autumn crocuses. Their leafless beauty had turned the drab yellow pasture into a picture more beautiful than anything I had seen before. But in a few sad hours the hot sun had burnt them up.

We sat down to breakfast on a stew, or *guiso*[3] as it is called, with *choclos*[4] or maize eaten off the cob. Afterwards the men went forth to rally more people to help to get us on the move again. They reckoned it would take thirty horses to do it, pulling in relays. We got home finally after eight hours of travelling and the death of one of the horses from heart failure. The going was more than a foot deep in sticky mud, and never have I seen horses so cruelly overworked. My pleas of mercy for them were ignored, for by the people out there horses are treated like machines and, when their working days are over, are left to die by the roadside and to be devoured by the vultures. Many times I have pleaded without success for a bullet to be put in the

[2] *Bichos*=insects.   [3] *Guiso* (stew). See also page 55.
[4] *Choclos*=corn-cobs.

brain of a moribund horse. Unfortunately, if one did it oneself, one would be liable to a heavy fine or imprisonment for killing somebody else's animal.

For a lover of horses the Argentine is the saddest place to live, for these most intelligent and willing animals and servants of men are never treated as they should be, but are roughly handled from the first. I think I learnt to speak fluent Spanish more quickly than usual because of my rages – as when, for example, I saw a brute of a man knock a horse's eye out with one lash, and then laugh. I learnt to upbraid them in no mild language; but all they said was that horses were worth only a few pesos, and they must be taught quickly. Hence the cruel method of breaking a horse in, by lashing it to make it gallop and then pulling it fiercely back on to its haunches, three men and horses all putting a concerted pull on its mouth at the same time. I pleaded with them to be kind, but it had no effect, so I decided to show them that I could break horses as quickly and as well as they could and without any cruelty. I begged the manager of the *estancia* to let me have a three year old to start on, but he refused point blank. 'Women don't break horses out here, that is a man's job,' he said, and all my pleading fell on deaf ears.

But I don't believe in being defeated in anything I really wish to do, so I bided my time. Shortly after this the whole of the unit went many miles away out into the camp on a branding job and were away for three days. The only people left were myself, my old Indian cook, and the old native who chopped our logs for us and did all the odd jobs such as butchering. I saw the men off, and then went out to the barn to find old Fernandez. I think he liked me, for I was the only person there who treated him like an ordinary human being and not as a slave. I asked him how long the *capitas* and *patrón* would be away, and he said, 'Three sun downs', so I told him that before they came back I wanted to break in a horse to do everything that their own horses could do. He looked at me as if I were mad, but

listened to me when I suggested that we should ride out in
the camp together to the wild herd and that he should lasso
one of the horses for me. I promised him tobacco and
pesos, and with much wagging of his head he agreed.

I could hardly wait whilst he ponderously saddled his fat
old mare and went to fetch a little bay pony for me. Together we rode out and at last came to the herd. At first they
paid no attention to us and we quietly rode round them.
Then I saw what I wanted, a beautiful golden chestnut with
four white socks and a blaze down her face. I pointed her
out to Fernandez but he shook his head. 'Don't have her,'
he said, 'she has a *mala cara*', which means a bad white
face, and in the eyes of the natives suggests a bad bargain
even before you start. But I knew this to be nonsense, and
told him to catch her. Neatly the rope encircled her neck,
and then she flung herself about like a salmon on a line.
But eventually she was tied to the ring in the saddle of his
own horse, and his old mount played the youngster like an
experienced fisherman. Bit by bit she stopped pulling, and
in the end we got her tied up near the house on a rawhide
halter and a rope. By this time the old man was terrified
of what he'd done and begged me to let her go again, for he
said the master would kill him when he came home. I told
him it was nonsense; that Englishmen didn't behave like
that, and that I myself would take full responsibility. And
in any case I had heard the *patrón* telling him before he
left to do all that I wanted. Miserably he slunk off to his
barn to continue his routine task of scraping the fat and
flesh off the sheep skins to make them ready for the
tannery. I could hardly believe my luck. Here was this
gorgeous creature for me to tame, and no one to say me
nay.

I approached her gently, speaking in a low caressing tone
of voice. She flinched at first on my approach and snorted
furiously, but did nothing more. I then stroked her nose and
her neck, and ran my fingers gently down her mane, for I
knew that horses loved this, and soon she stood quite

dreamily still; so I then ran my hands down her legs and picked up her feet, talking gently and soothingly all the time. Next I went down her body and picked up her back legs; then round the other side and back to her head. Then I got a sack and gently slapped her all over with it. She leapt in the air with the first feel of it, but soon, when she found it did not hurt her, she paid no more attention to it. I whisked it over her back and under her tummy. I slapped her legs gently, and down her tail. I then dropped the sack off her back until she no longer flinched, and that ended the first lesson. Next I taught her to eat sugar by putting it between her back teeth. At first she spat it out, so the next time I held it in her mouth until it had nearly melted. That worked wonderfully, and in no time she was crunching up as much as I could give her. But I kept it as a reward for everything new that I wished to teach her. I next fetched my saddle and put it on her back with a very loose girth. Up went her back in a terrific buck, but I talked to her and moved the saddle about, and then tightened the girth one hole and made her move. This time she hunched her back but did not buck, so I tightened it up to make it safe, and then got an old wood block and put it by her side, so that I could stand on it and lean heavily over her, talking all the while. She never stirred, so gently I swung my leg over her and slid on and off about three times like this. I then put reins on the side pieces of her head-collar, since I do not believe in bits, and I sat on her back whilst she was still tied up. Next I urged her forwards a pace or two, and then said 'Ssh' and pulled her to a stop on the reins. Encouraged by her docility I slipped off the rope she was tied up with, and leant over to pull her gently on the head-collar to urge her forward. She walked on, and after half an hour of this I unsaddled her and took her out into the small paddock by the house and tied the long rope to a movable tree trunk and let her wander. At first she was terrified of the log moving along after her, but soon she got accustomed to it. After lunch I brought her in again

TAMING A PONY

*Approaching an unbroken pony, breathing gently
down my nostrils*

The pony approaches me

The 'How do you do'

Friends

The pony meets a shoe for the first time

Off we go, hold tight!

The breathing 'How do you do' works with cattle too

and rode her for another half an hour. Soon she was trotting and walking well, but I still had the feeling that she might panic at any minute.

Anyway, to cut a long story short, by the end of the three days this pony was going extremely well. I opened the gates of the corral, told old Fernandez to follow me at a distance, and off I went on her for my first ride. It was without incident for some time, until something frightened her in the grass, when she put herself into a series of bucks that would have done credit to a buck-jumping contest. I was ready for it, for all the time she had felt to me as if the slightest error on my part would make her try to get rid of me. However, we came home safely, and I caressed her lovingly and let her free in the small paddock near the house. Next morning I rode alone for an hour, and so her breaking continued smoothly.

On the last day before the men came home, I met an old Guarani Indian,[5] riding a beautiful little bay mare. We stopped and said polite things to each other, and I told him I was taming the chestnut I was on. He said he thought only his own tribe knew the secret of taming horses without fear, and, when asked what it was, he told me to watch the next time I turned strange horses out together and see what they did. I asked what he meant, and he told me that horses always go up to each other and sniff each other's noses, which is their way of saying 'How do you do?' in their language, and that he always did the same thing when he wished to tame a horse himself. He said: 'Stand with your hands behind your back and blow gently down through your nostrils. Keep quite still, and the horse will come up to you and sniff and will blow up your own nose, after which all fear will have left him. That horse, providing that you don't give it reason to turn vicious, will always be your friend and the friend of man.' And with

[5] Guarani: peaceable tribe of South American Indians, having their home chiefly in Paraguay and Uruguay and on the Brazilian coast.

that he cantered off at the easy gallop of the perfectly matched horse and rider, with his reins hanging loosely and without a saddle, just a blanket on the horse's back.

That evening the men came home and I told them what I had been up to, and of course got the most severe scolding possible. Fernandez was threatened with the sack, but I pointed out that it was my fault entirely and that he had been ordered to do what I wanted. No more was said until I gave a little show with my *mala cara*, who behaved like a lamb, and the manager said he supposed I could break a horse. I felt this was the moment to ask for another, for I was dying to try out the Guarani's trick. So another was caught up for me. I sniffed up her nose and immediately stroked her and saddled her up. From her behaviour she might have been an old horse, for she never flinched or snorted or showed any sign of fear. I cut out the preliminary sack flapping and fondling and gently mounted her, loosed the rope, and with my heels urged her on. She went smoothly with me, and I never for a second had that feeling that I had had with the other horse, that at any minute she and I might part company. In twenty minutes in the corral I taught her to stop, and to turn, and to trot, and then I asked the men watching me to open the gate and away we went. In an hour she was cantering, turning, stopping, and allowing me to mount and dismount without any protest or signs of fear.

I knew the Indian was right, for that horse never put a foot wrong and in three days was a completely trained pony. I could safely round up cattle with her, open and shut gates, and so on; and all this on a head-collar only. I never bitted my horses until much later on, when I knew that they knew what to do from my voice alone. I have won many a bet in England that I would do anything normal on a horse without saddle or bridle, winning simply because I knew that my horse knew every command of voice. For a bet, I have played fast polo on reins of one strand of '50' cotton. My success with the Guarani's trick gave me the chance in life I had always wanted, for from now on, instead of the *peons* being paid to tame the horses, they were given more useful jobs, like fencing, to do, and I was promoted to be horse-breaker at ten shillings per horse. The Inspector of the cattle company was told about me and came out later to see why a woman was allowed to do this. He rode one of my horses that had been completely untouched two hours before and could find no fault in it except lack of experience. It was thus that I became the happiest woman on earth in my self-chosen job.

5 Taming Horses
     in the Argentine

About three months after the Director's visit, a letter was delivered by hand to the manager from the area manager instructing us to move that very day to take over another *estancia*, in quite a different part of the country.

Nothing pleases me more than to get a move on, but this unnecessary move without any warning struck me as being just red tape. Here we were having to gather up our entire personnel with all their worldly goods, all our domestic livestock, maids and their belongings, and set off to take over another *estancia* about eighty miles away! The manager, however, was delighted, for it was promotion for him apparently, and the new *estancia* was much nearer civilization. The railway ran through it and there was a little village only a league away, so as far as he was concerned everything in the garden was lovely.

Our old cook wasn't too happy about leaving the place she had lived in so long, but she didn't think it would be right to leave me unchaperoned, so with much grumbling all her belongings went into a sack. Nor did her daughter want to leave her other unmarried sister who lived in the neighbourhood, so they were both invited to come along too. After all, they were paid only about five shillings a week each anyway.

Dawn was around three in the morning, and then hustle and bustle started everywhere. One could hear the clucking of frightened chickens and the fury of turkeys and ducks as they were all hustled into wooden crates and stacked under the great farm wagon that was to move the household. We had one farm wagon for the domestic side of the move and two more for the *estancia* essentials. They were huge wagons, each drawn by six horses, but in spite of their size they seemed to me terribly overloaded, and it was agonizing to see the horses struggle to get the wagons started.

I rode as usual with faithful Fernandez to accompany me. In the wagon were old Maria and her two daughters, with the foreman's wife and her three babies. Fernandez and I rode behind. The manager had gone on with the foreman, some hours before, on horseback. With us, all went smoothly for the first forty miles, but when we arrived at a river, the wagon driver instead of asking Fernandez to go ahead and see how deep it was, just shouted for all he was worth and lashed the horses, who sprang straight into the water, which was far too deep for them. Within seconds they were swimming for their lives, with the wagon floundering hopelessly, and its occupants up to their waists in water even though they were already standing up. They were holding the babies above their heads, and the household goods were floating around everywhere. The horses succeeded in reaching the other side, but pull as they might they couldn't get the wagon up the slope out of the river. The driver thrashed them mercilessly until I yelled to him to stop and then plunged my horse into the river and snatched the whip from the brute's hand. He knew he was himself to blame and was venting his anger on the horses. I told Fernandez to go and get help while we did our best to keep the horses quiet. The wagon was safely grounded on the river bed, but of course all the poultry that had been slung under it were drowning. I went back into the water two or three times to rescue floating articles, my arab Wendy appearing to enjoy her swim. It seemed ages before Fernandez returned with three men and horses to pull us out, his own horse being attached to the wagon with his lasso. What a sorry sight everything was! Every blanket was drenched, all the clothes the travellers possessed were wringing wet, and there were still about forty miles to travel before reaching the new *estancia*. I spoke to the men who had come to our aid, and they invited the caval-cade to stop at their *puesta* further on to dry out. It was sad to see all the dead poultry, and amongst them the two geese which had been real friends to me, though I fear I did not regret the foreman's turkey cock! He had been a vile bird and his angry red face had kept the other poultry and the foreman's dog completely under his rule for years without number.

We rode on with the wagon and its occupants as far as the *puesta*, and then I left them, for I too was soaking wet, and it was by no means warm. It took us six long hours more ride to the new home. We stopped only once to give the horses a drink, and an old señora rushed out to offer me her maté pot, which I dared not refuse. But I certainly said a prayer for the future state of my health when I drank from it! The old señor came out too and admired my Wendy. He said he would like to buy a foal of hers, if ever she had one, and then he asked me if I'd like to see his yearlings. I gathered that this was a great district for Sunday race meetings, all the neighbouring landowners competing, and he showed me one glorious bay pony that he kept in a tumbledown shack. It was all rugged up with sacks, and he told me he fed it on maize and alfalfa and that it had won ninety races already. Had I not been so wet I should have liked to talk to him much longer, for he obviously knew a great deal about horses. But we had to get on with our journey, so I waved goodbye, and the whole family came out to wish us 'Hasta la vista' ('Until we meet again').

By this time I was beginning to get badly rubbed, with my wet clothes against the English saddle, and it made me appreciate the quality of the native saddles that they use out there. These consist first of all of a mackintosh covered with a woollen blanket; then two panels of stuffed leather kept together with leather thongs like a corset, so that the size can be altered to fit any horse. The pads fit snugly on each side of the backbone, and are covered with a natural sheepskin, and on top of it all goes a wart hog's skin which is beautifully soft. The idea of these saddles is that a man is thus able to carry with him everything that he is likely to need for weeks in the open. The mackintosh goes on the ground, when he is making his bed in the open, and on that goes the woollen blanket. Then the leather pads make his pillow, and his big *poncho*, without which no Argentine rider of the range would ever travel, finally covers him over completely. No rain, however heavy, ever penetrates a *poncho*. When a man is riding, if the weather is fine, the *poncho* is tied in a roll in front of his saddle; but if it rains it is worn buttoned high up to the neck, and used like this it covers the horse as well.

I was getting into a state of utter misery and discomfort, so I tried to ride side-saddle for a few miles, a rather risky procedure without a pommel. However, Wendy knew that she had to be very careful, and it certainly helped me. At last we arrived, and the excitement at getting there made me forget how sore and weary I was.

The *estancia* house was on a hill and could be seen from some distance away, and the country was quite different from what I was accustomed to. There were wizened trees which bore flowers very much like mimosa and had an intoxicating scent. Parrots shrieked from the palm trees, and there were streams everywhere, shallow and easy to ford. However, the water in them is not always so low. There was one stream that ran at the bottom of the *estancia* which was a mere trickle on the day we arrived, but I remember that some months later, when we had a terrific storm, in a few minutes it had become a roaring flood. You can judge from what follows how quickly that happened. A traveller who was delivering a new car to a customer was passing through it just before the storm came, when the car stalled in mid-stream and the man got out to walk to our *estancia* – ten minutes' walk at the outside – to ask for a horse to pull him out. But by the time we were able to get a horse ready and get back to the car its roof was the only thing visible. The roaring raging torrent had widened the river to fifty yards and no horse could have lived in it. This spate lasted for three weeks and the car became a total loss.

Well, to get back to our arrival at our new home. It was late evening already, and I was hoping that the manager or the foreman would have got a fire going and a kettle boiling ready for tea, but when we arrived the place was just a bare shell. In this district, apparently, wood for fuel has to be brought from a long distance and the outgoing manager had left none. But it takes a woman to make a home, and in no time I had scouted round and found some old boxes and had got a fire going and a cup of tea ready. I had to dry my own things on me, as all the trunks containing our clothes were coming on the other wagons by a different way, and the wild horses were being driven along with them. I was glad they weren't attempting to come the way we had come ourselves.

This new *estancia* consisted of three rooms in the main house, and kitchen quarters and, joy of joys, a bathroom with a modern bath! Then there was another part which provided an office, and a very large room which the manager had for himself. The foreman's cottage was fifty yards away and nearly as comfortable as the main house. I wondered what *his* bath would be used for. All around the house were tangerine trees and excitedly I picked the luscious fruits and ate them. They were much more delicious than any I had ever tasted before, and I ate many of them. On the house grew geraniums of all kinds, pink ones and red ones, and round about there was a vegetable garden with everything in it that one expected to find in an ordinary English garden. My mind flew to the cookery book, and to all the things that I should now be able to make. But how much more I should have enjoyed my first sight of this new home if I hadn't been so cold!

Fairly soon after we had got there, the poor people in the

flooded wagon also arrived; they were very tired, but surprisingly cheerful. I have never known more charming, simple people. Their wants were few and they became such faithful friends. Their first thoughts were for me, but I assured them that I was all right. Luckily I had the kettle ready boiling for them, and the foreman had slaughtered a lamb and a roast was being prepared outside. Soon they were sipping their maté, and before long we all settled down to the coldest night we'd spent for a long time. The blankets were soaking wet, and it wasn't until the sun came out next day that we were able to dry them at all. The first thing that old Maria and her daughters did next day was to go down to the little stream and wash everything that had got dirty on the journey. I went down to see what they were doing, and was astounded to see them pounding everything between stones in the running water. Then they laid it all out on the grass to dry, and never had I seen more spotless things, when they had finished! I shall never understand why everything wasn't in holes in a few minutes, but in the two years I was there I never saw even the finest underclothes in any way harmed by this treatment.

Old Maria's daughter Valentina used to amuse me by catching fish in the stream with her hands. But it did mean that we could always have fish for a meal when we wanted to. The fish she caught were delicious little fish rather like sprats, and she must have pounced like lightning to grab them so quickly – certainly no one else could do it.

Just beside the river some distance from the *estancia* was a swampy area covered with very green grass, and it was here that we lost the horse for the 'sulky',[1] soon after we arrived. It was a horribly impressive as well as a saddening incident, for until I had this demonstration of the powerlessness of muscle and bone against the dreadful suction of the bog, I had felt, as many do, that by the exertion of courage and utmost physical effort, escape might be made

[1] A light two-wheeled one-horse vehicle.

possible. Our 'sulky' horse was not as fortunate as the little pony whose adventure I am about to relate. This working horse had gone to graze the lovely green patch, which looked so inviting after the burnt-up pasture he had been used to, but he met a terrifyingly quick death in the treacherous swamp before anyone could get a rope round his neck to pull him out. It was dreadful to see the helpless creature die in this way, and, as a good 'sulky' horse is a rarity, his loss was also a tragedy for us all. Apparently there were many such dangerous swamps, and, unless one can get a rope round the animal's neck quickly, a horse or a cow is sucked right under in no time. Our own horses came from a part of the country where these swamps didn't exist, so they were always having to be pulled out. I remember that soon after we got there, I was riding a pony one day that I had only just started to break, when without warning her back legs went down and we began to sink rapidly. My only hope of safety was to climb over her head onto some dry grass that I could see ahead, and then try to pull her out. Fortunately, she trusted me implicitly, and I prayed that she wouldn't struggle or our days would be over for both of us. She was sinking steadily, but did nothing as I climbed up her neck and over her head onto firm ground. Then I urged her to try to get out. I pulled with desperate strength, and she struggled valiantly with me, only resting when I did. Little by little we won through, and finally with an almighty heave she got her front feet onto firm ground and then pulled herself out. We were both of us gasping for breath and I was thankful at that moment for the bond of trust there was between us. She knew I would try my hardest to save her life and so she did just as I wanted. Slowly and carefully we rode home, and from that day on she was one of my favourite horses. I was sad indeed when later on the manager claimed her and gave her to a man to train as a racing pony. She was extraordinarily fast and won many of the Sunday races for him, but she was worth more than that to me as a mount.

That was the heartbreaking business of being official horsebreaker, for I loved them all and never wanted to part with them to the *peons* who treated them so differently from me. All my wages went in buying for myself as many of them as I could afford.

At this time I was taming about four of them every week. They were caught up from the herd for me, I breathed a welcome up their noses, telling them gently all I wanted them to do, and they submitted themselves to me almost immediately. I never spoke to them above a whisper, for I know that animals like a quiet voice, and if you are in tune with them it just doesn't matter what words you actually use. It is the intonation of voice that matters, and one's thoughts are transmitted in some mysterious way through the touch of one's fingers or directly from mind to mind. Time and time again I have proved this when out riding, by just thinking silently of which way to go, and finding that the pony almost invariably takes the right turning. My cows now do the same. I have a choice of three paddocks for them when they come out of the cowshed, and without any help from me my old thirteen-year-old one always makes her way to the pasture that I want her to take. I think one has to be within about twenty-five yards of them to transmit this telepathic control, but that it happens there can be no doubt.

It is very much the same thing when I am upset or angry, for the animals always know without a word being spoken when I am unhappy, perhaps, or ill, or if I am out of temper. I now make it a rule never to go near my horses to attempt to tame them, if I am cross about anything, for my irritability communicates itself to them at once, and then that communion is lost which is so essential if one is to make them do what one wants them to do, instantly and without fear.

6   South-American Jean

My first thought, when we had settled down in this new *estancia*, was to send for my Great Dane Jean, whom I had had to leave in England; so I cabled my mother asking her to put the dog on the next boat out, and saying that I would meet her in Buenos Aires, as we were now living only a few miles from the junction station and I could easily go down to meet her alone. I had not dared to bring her out with me, not knowing what I was coming to, for I felt that she would die when put into quarantine, if I had to return to England. This *estancia* kept more sheep than cattle and I looked forward to teaching my dog to work the sheep. She used to understand every word I spoke and I felt that with her I would have a wonderful time. It thus came about five weeks later that I left the *estancia* for the first time for over eighteen months to visit civilization once more.

I got to the docks many hours too early, and was tremendously excited when I saw the ship in the distance waiting to dock. When at last she came into the quay, I could see Jean standing by the rail, being held by some strange lady. When I whistled to her she went nearly mad, and I thought for a moment that she would jump over the rails. It had been a silly thing for me to do, but I longed to make sure at once that she had not forgotten me. In no time she came down the gangway, and there was no holding her. She bounded into my arms, nearly knocking me down, and I got a complete bath of kisses. Then I noticed that she was lame on a back leg and I asked what had happened. I was told that a drunken sailor had kicked her, and I could see that although the wound had healed she was still lame, which worried me dreadfully. She never did get quite right again after that, but fortunately it didn't seem to bother her at all.

I took her off to the hotel where I was staying the night and she clung to me as if she daren't shut an eye for fear that I should disappear again. She was tremendously admired by everyone, for I don't think anyone there had ever seen a Great Dane before. I had to go to the railway office to get special permission to take her on the train with me and to get the train to stop at the *estación*,[1] which they would do by arrangement in those days, as they had very few passengers. But to my dismay, when I got to the station, I found the guard most unwilling to have her on the train at all. I promised, however, to stay with her in the guard's van all the time to make sure she did him no harm, and this seemed to satisfy him. On the way, when we were on the ferry, I took her for a walk round it, and the dining-car assistants gave her a good meal of meat. Eventually we arrived at our destination and were met by old Fernandez in the 'sulky'. Jean jumped up at once and sat bolt upright beside me, taking everything in, and every now and then she gave me a big lick on an unsuspecting cheek. It seemed as if she just wanted to keep on telling me how much she loved me! When we arrived everyone rushed out to greet us and to admire Jean; but alas, she wouldn't greet the manager, and so to him she was a stupid dog. I tried my best to persuade her to be friendly with him, but no, she dropped her tail, and looked miserable. Later I knew that she was right, as animals always are.

I soon taught Jean to be a first-class sheep dog and we took over some of the work with the sheep. It was good for the horses I was breaking to have some definite work to carry out, and Jean used to go down to the gullies to pick up any lambs that had fallen down, which she would then bring up in her mouth. Only a Great Dane could have

[1] *Estación*=station.

done that. I used then to sling the lambs in front of me on my horse and take them back to the *estancia*, as most of them were found to be injured in some way or other.

One day, when I went out to the flock, a ghastly sight met my eyes. Some killer dogs had been at work and dead and dying sheep were to be seen everywhere. I knew that I must go back to the *estancia* immediately to get help, but if I were to leave the sheep unguarded the birds of prey would peck and kill those that were not yet dead, and the killer dogs might return. So I tried to explain to Jean that she must stay and guard them until I came back. She seemed to understand what I wanted, in her quiet way, and to show me that I need not worry she lay down and closed her eyes as if in sleep. When I went away, for as far as my sight would carry I kept turning back to watch what she was doing, and whenever I looked back I saw her beautiful head still held upright and that she was still watching me and never moving at all. It took me seven hours altogether to get help, for there was no one at home when I reached the *estancia* and I had to go out to find the men where they were working. I was much worried as to how Jean would feel in the terrible heat of the day, as she was not accustomed to such high temperatures, but when we got back eventually, she was just where I had left her, and I don't think she had moved more than fifty yards in the course of her duties. The sheep were grazing quietly, and those that had been hurt had suffered no further harm from the vultures. How glad Jean was to see me, and to have a drink and some meat that I had brought for her! I then left the men to their heartbreaking task of slaughtering the injured, and wound my own weary way home.

One day, as I was taking my siesta on the *patio*, I heard shouting from the foreman's cottage and his little boy came running up to say that the locusts were coming. Everyone panicked, shutting all the doors and running about banging sheets of tin or anything else that they could lay hands on. Jean thought it meant burglars, and I

am sure that her bark must have frightened many of them
away! But soon it became almost dark with them and the
ground was literally covered. Towards nightfall the locusts
climbed up off the ground and clung to the trunks of trees
or anything else they could cling to, and the ponies ate
them ravenously. Jean ate some too, but didn't seem to
think them very tasty. It appears that locusts always climb
up the trees in the evening, if they can, and get their wings
wet with dew during the night's rest. They then descend
again in the morning, when their wings are dry, and go on
eating everything in sight. Our own plague stayed to lay
their eggs, and soon there were millions more of them in
the crawling stage. These the men tried to slaughter by
digging great pits for them, when they were on the move,
and then pouring petrol over them and burning them up.
When we got rid of them at last the camp was seen to be
completely bare, and the sheep with their lambs were soon
in a desperate plight. The losses were terrible. It is a fright-
ful thing that in that part of the country, where no special
crops are grown as extra food for the animals in an emergency, the cattle and sheep must starve to death if severe
drought comes or a plague of locusts. On this occasion
some of the flocks were sent elsewhere as quickly as possible, but the sheep were so weak by then that many of
them died in transit.

It was great fun having a little village only three miles
away, and I often used to ride there on my pony, with Jean
for company, to do the shopping. I was always puzzled by
the terror my pony showed when we got to a certain spot
in the road about half-way there. She seemed to refuse to go
on without much soothing and quite firm handling on
my part, and Jean also showed her obvious uneasiness and
her hair would stand up all the way down her back. I
told the villagers about this and I found out that the road
had been made through an old Jewish cemetery, and it was
the ghosts of the Jews that were supposed to be haunting
it. This seemed to confirm the theory that animals have a

sixth sense and can see things we ourselves cannot see, and the uneasiness of my own animals, when we passed that way, certainly made me feel very creepy. I think there must have been some exceptionally conscienceless evildoer buried there, for surely an animal would not be so deeply affected at passing a burial ground, if it were not haunted by some earthbound spirit – but one knows so little about what animals can sense and fear.

After one extremely hot day, we had all just settled down to our evening meal when the *estancia* dogs set up such a noise that Jean leaped up to add to the furore with her own booming bark. We went to the door and discovered a cavalcade of horses, dogs and children approaching. There is an unwritten law in the Argentine, known as the 'sundowners' law', which makes it absolutely necessary to give board and lodging to any traveller who needs it from sundown to sunrise – and here our hospitality was wanted with a vengeance! The party consisted of an old father and mother and seven children, not to mention innumerable dogs and horses. So with smiles hiding our dismay at such an invasion we went to greet our guests. We gave instructions for a roast lamb to be got ready and maté pots were soon steaming and the whole family making polite conversation round our fireside. It was as much as I could do to stand the smell of their unwashed bodies, not to mention the expert spitting into the fire of old papa.

The children were fascinated by my canaries, and before I could say a word the poor little hen had been frightened off her eggs. Her eyes and those of her mate became little black pinpoints of terror, and I had to take her into my bedroom and to speak soothingly to them both before the little cock would give me his usual bright 'cheep, cheep'. The little hen needed even more comforting. So I took her out of her cage and pressed her little beak to my mouth and kissed her, as her poor little breast panted up and down. This I feel is a bird's language: so many species caress each other with their beaks – perhaps it is a reminder of the nestlings being fed by the parent birds. She soon realized that she was safe, so I gently returned her to her nest. She then looked at me as if to say 'thank you', fluffed out her wings until she looked double her normal size, and settled off to sleep, and to dream of her future family.

On returning to the bedlam in the sitting-room I found papa, with the help of a bottle of *caña*,[2] becoming very companionable. His stories of his wins on the racecourse were becoming more exaggerated every minute. Mama was suckling her youngest baby unashamedly, and the other children were still rampaging about. I made wild dashes here and there to save my odds and ends, but in the twinkling of an eye the inkpot was over the carpet, a picture came hurtling down, and Jean had slunk off outdoors. So I blessed the moment when the foreman announced that the meal was ready at last. Knives were then drawn from their sheaths, and the family went out to eat its fill. I myself said good night and expressed the hope they would sleep well in the office room which had been made ready for them. On the following morning, after many pretty speeches, the whole noisy family moved on.

So the summer passed. I was happy in my work, my horses were tamed by love and kindness, and I believe that the natives themselves on this *estancia* were beginning to treat their own horses better. I found that the news had spread around the countryside that a woman broke horses there, and I used to get stared at rather strangely wherever I went.

It was not many months after the locust invasion that I began to feel ill – I lost my appetite and was constantly sick. I didn't pay much attention to this at first, but I soon began to lose weight at an alarming speed, and to feel very weak, so I arranged to have myself taken by road into the town to see a native doctor, who arranged for urine and blood tests to be made. The results showed that I had a

[2] *Caña*=sugar-cane distilled.

five per cent glycosuria,[3] and he diagnosed diabetes. This meant that I had to take insulin and to suffer the terrible business of jabbing the stuff into my leg twice a day. Sometimes I went almost into a coma as a result of it and had to take sugar to make myself better. To cut a long story short, before very long I knew I was dying, and in a matter of a few weeks I became a living skeleton and practically blind, and the doctor said he could do nothing more for me. As a result of all this, I think I must have gone slightly mental, my own idea now being to go out into the pampas to die. I knew that there was an extremely wicked horse in the barn that had thrown some of the *peons* very badly, and I thought that if only that horse would kill me I should then suffer no more. So, one day, when everyone had gone out I got my saddle and bridle, and very, very slowly I went out to the barn where the horse was kept. No one saw me go, for even my old cook had left two days before on some unknown mission. I went up to the black horse and again very slowly and with much effort saddled him up. Jean whined plaintively in the meantime, as if she knew I was doing wrong. I then climbed up the side of the box and into the saddle, trembling like a leaf all the time with fatigue. The horse moved off obediently. I urged him on faster as best I could, but he would do no more than break into the gentlest of trots. He went wherever I willed, and if he'd been the gentlest of horses he could not have behaved more beautifully. In that moment I realized once again that animals are always right, and I knew that I had been wicked even to have hoped that this beautiful creature might kill me. Slowly I rode him home. I was completely exhausted and he bore me along slowly and more gently than I could ever have imagined. I could no longer guide him myself, but he knew where to go and he brought me safely home. As we reached the *estancia* I saw that everyone was in a tremendous flurry, looking for me everywhere, but I was able to say nothing in explanation

[3] A condition in which sugar appears in the urine.

as they helped me into the house.

That night my old cook returned. She had been to see the Indians where she used to live, for she thought they knew a cure for diabetes. She had brought with her the fresh growing twigs of the Sarandi Blanco tree,[4] and was soon cutting them into small pieces about four inches long and infusing them in hot water. The result was a pale green liquid which she begged me to drink. I felt it could do no harm in the circumstances, so I drank it, and then fell into a deep sleep. Next morning she brought me another dose and begged me not to give myself any more insulin, for she said that this remedy would cure me by itself. I obeyed her, for I had little to lose, and I took a glass of this daily for a week, soon beginning to feel better, and to be able to manage all right without the insulin. In three weeks I was feeling quite a different person and I knew I was getting well. She now told me to take a glass of the potion only every other day, instead of every day, and still with no ill results. Every day I got better and six weeks later I decided to stop the treatment altogether. This seemed to have no ill effects whatever, and from that day to this I have had no return of the illness. This treatment depends on having the young shoots of the tree, for the old twigs have no effect. Later, I and other English people brought bundles of the twigs home for an old Colonel who had had diabetes for forty-seven years: in three days he was able to give up his insulin, but had to continue drinking a glass of the infusion every day, which suggests that it cures diabetes in the

---

[4] The botanical name for the Sarandi Blanco tree is *Phyllanthus sellowianus* (Müller Arg.) from the botanical family of Euphorbiaceae. It is a small tree or shrub measuring from 1.50 to 4.00 metres in height, and growing naturally in South America in corridors or galleries and along the riverside of the Paraná, Uruguay and La Plata rivers. It is also to be found in Misiones, Entre Rios, Corrientes, Santa Fé, and on the island of Martín Garcia. I am indebted for this information to Captain V. Boyle, C.M.G., M.R.C.V.S., Veterinary Officer, British Embassy, Buenos Aires.

early stages, but only replaces the insulin in cases of long standing. But how much pleasanter the potion than jabbing a needle into oneself all the time!

Another drug commonly used in the Argentine and not found in England is Esculeol, a liquid of which forty drops are taken every day for not more than ten days, which is a wonderful cure for piles and varicose veins. I intend one day to get some more of it over here to find out exactly what it is.

I was persuaded to go back to England now that I was stronger, for fear that anything should go wrong again. So I had to pack up, meaning to return later on to my beloved dog and my horses. I hated the thought of leaving them all, although I knew my old cook would love Jean like a child. One day I had gone to speak to them in their room, and I found the two maids lying asleep on the floor and Jean in their bed with her head on the pillow. When I asked them what on earth they were doing, they said the floor was too hard for 'poor Jean'!

The last weeks before I left for England were hell. Jean knew I was going away and used to lie with her head on my suitcase, her pitiful eyes begging for comfort. There were only two courses that I could take. One was to put her to sleep then and there, the other to leave her with Maria until my return, for I never thought then that I would never return. Years later, I discovered from a man who came on leave from the same *estancia* that the manager had never put Jean to sleep as I had asked, so my mind has never since ceased being tortured by not knowing her end. She had hated him on sight, and I never ought to have trusted him to carry out my wishes.

7   Horse-dealing Housewife

It was not for some months after my return to England that I really felt my old self again. I was staying at home with my mother, and it was a horse that once more gave me an interest in life.

When an old horse-dealing friend of mine, who had helped me in the past to buy horses for my riding-school, heard from my mother that I was at home again, he called in to see me, and after we had been chatting for a short time told me that he had really come to see me because he knew of a horse that was 'just my sort'. Well, when old Bill Organ said that, I knew what he meant. He never made a mistake where a horse was concerned, so I said we'd go and see it, although I didn't feel strong enough yet to ride. So off we set, and we went to a farm in the country. There an extremely horsy individual brought out the most beautiful bay pony, and of course I fell in love with it straight away. He began telling me all about it, including its age, until my companion nudged him and reminded him that what I didn't know about horses wasn't worth knowing, and that a twelve-year-old horse couldn't lose six years quite as easily as that. However, I bought the pony and next day it came home. From the moment it arrived a new spirit seemed to enter into me. We loved each other on sight, and so it was that I started riding again.

He had a hard mouth, but in no time at all I got him to behave by teaching him to listen to my words and not to rely on my reins. I always train my horses with the same words. 'Sssh' for stop, 'wee trot', 'wee canter', and 'this way', putting out a hand for whichever way I wish the horse to go. I use the word 'wee' because it has what I call a high-pitched note which is easily picked up by the horse and attracts his attention: the 'sssh' is a soothing sound to make them stop. And of course by putting out one's hand to the right or left the horse learns to neck rein easily, and in my opinion no horse can be a joy to ride if it won't neck rein properly. I now rode this beautiful creature daily, calling him Cracker because he was always wanting to do everything with such a bang. I trained him until the weakest child could have ridden him. He didn't want reins, just a voice. But when I had had him about six weeks, I heard of an elderly lady who wanted a perfect hack, and decided to offer her Cracker, for my funds were running low and I felt that, if I could get him a good home and make a profit on him, he ought to go.

She came down and tried him and it was a foregone conclusion that she would have him. I made a fair profit. Then once more I consulted my pal Bill Organ and we went off horse-dealing. We soon found a heavyweight unbroken cob of about 15.2, that had been reared on a farm and was untouched. I bought it for twenty pounds and got it home that same morning, I breathed up its nose, saddled it up, and with a fair amount of encouragement got it moving. In an hour it was going like a lamb, and was already extremely comfortable to ride. After lunch I decided to clip it out, removing all its long coat. The transformation was astounding, for there, after clipping, was the perfect heavyweight hunter. It was while I was in the middle of this clipping operation that a strange man and his wife turned up and said they'd been told I had a horse for sale. I supposed they meant Cracker, although I couldn't think how they'd heard about him, and I told them that I'd sold him. They greatly admired the horse I was titivating up. I told them I'd bought it only that morning, but that in my opinion it was already completely safe. The lady said her husband was looking for a horse just like that and asked if they could try it. I said, yes, at their own risk. The old boy got up, and off amongst the traffic he went. He came back and said: 'How much?' I replied 'Sixty pounds,' and the deal was done. They wrote to me several times afterwards to say what a perfect animal it was. So all was well.

I was lost without a horse, so I went down to a local horse-dealer, as my old pal Organ hadn't anything in mind that day. I looked round the stables and saw a rather vicious-looking liver chestnut. All horse-dealers, including incidentally the Argentinos, dislike a liver chestnut, and they say that a good one has yet to be born. Goodness knows why! The owner of this one told me it was a 'bit of a swine' and left it at that, but when I bid him twenty-six pounds for it, he slapped my hand as quickly as he could and the deal was done. I borrowed a saddle and bridle, which he said he'd pick up that afternoon, and away I went. This certainly was a horrid creature, if ever there was one. One felt that every lamp-post might be a possible rubbing-off post, and I had to ride him home with more care than I had taken with a horse for many a year. When I got home, we went into the orchard, where he set off with his head practically on the ground, and a mouth of iron, straight for an apple tree. I was to be rubbed off, but by bending low I just succeeded in foiling him.

I stopped to think. This brute's mouth was like iron: very well, I'd put him on a head-collar only. So I removed the bit, breathed up his nose, and mounted again. I began to teach him by words, and bit by bit his wilfulness left him, with the result that in less than an hour he became a lovely ride. I put him in the stable and later I clipped him out. Next day the horse-dealer came for his saddle and found me grooming the horse which, with his mane off, looked quite different. Years ago I had mastered the art of tail pulling, and I could make a horse look very nice. The dealer said: 'Nice horse you have there,' obviously not recognizing it as his own. I replied, 'Yes, do you want to buy it?' He said he'd like a ride on it, so I saddled it up, with my tongue well in my cheek. He took it out, and it behaved as a nice horse should. When he came in and offered me twenty pounds profit, I said, 'I sell this horse to you without any warranty whatsoever.' His reply was that he knew a good 'un when he saw one, and he took out his cheque book and wrote out a cheque. I wondered whether the joke had gone far enough; but I thought I'd teach him a lesson, for he'd often boasted that he would recognize a horse anywhere. He took the horse home, and I heard nothing. The next thing I heard was that he'd won the hunter trials on it, and it wasn't until weeks later when I met him that I asked him if I could have my horse back. 'Not on your life,' he said, 'it is the best jumper I've ever owned.' I couldn't resist telling him now that it was his own horse, and never have I seen such a silly look on a man's face. He held out his hand and said, 'Well, I don't know,' and he shook me warmly by the hand saying that he'd never have believed the horse he sold me could have been the horse I sold him. But nevertheless it was.

I wasn't always so successful. Old Organ and I both got taken in by a gipsy, who sold me a glorious horse that seemed sound in every way, but which had been given a dose of lead shot[1] just before I saw it, a ruse that masks a broken wind for a few days. I was told after that to give a drink of cold water to any suspected 'loaded horse', as that would show the trick up for what it was.

It was whilst I was gaining momentum with buying and selling horses that my sister, who was a school teacher, fell ill. The school were desperately trying to find a substitute, so I offered my services. I'd no academic qualifications except in agriculture, but I thought I could amuse small children, and that's what most schools should do in my opinion. The headmistress was very grateful, and I think

---

[1] A weight of lead shot or of grease in the stomach, weighing it down, masks temporarily the uneven movement of the diaphragm symptomatic of broken wind – an old and successful trick of unscrupulous horse-dealers.

she was so impressed by my sports Wolseley that she forgot to ask about my qualifications. I arrived next day and started off with the five to eight-year-olds. This was easy, for I soon invented tales about the letters of the alphabet, and I told them stories and made them paint what I had told them. In fact the morning flew. After break I was to take the older ones, and I decided that botany was now the answer. Here I was in my element, and after telling them things I took them out on a nature ramble. We brought home stacks of plants and grasses, and I kept them busy painting them and sticking them into their exercise books. While they were doing this I noticed a horse-dealer's yard opposite the school, and my eyes became glued to the window, for a beautiful youngster was being ridden out. In the break-time I shot over to the yard and made enquiries about it. I got on to it and then looked up at the form-room window. Horror of horrors! Those girls were all watching me! I felt I'd better wave, and they all waved back. Never before had their mistress ridden a horse in break-time. I bought the horse and told the dealer to send him to my home. Next day, I was so busy doing my horse that I was nearly late for school. I picked up what I thought was the history book I'd been swotting overnight so as to appear to know at least something, and rushed into school just as the bell went. I went into the bigger girls' form room and with a prim 'Good morning, girls', sat down to read all about the Wars of the Roses. Alas, in my hurry I'd picked up not a history book but *Mr Pinkerton, Detective*. I told the girls what I'd done and said that if they promised to be very quiet I'd read it to them. Silence reigned, and when I left the classroom the headmistress met me and said how very well I managed the girls, and that never had she heard them so quiet. If only she'd known why!

I am afraid the curriculum at this school suffered sadly under my guidance. The girls grew well versed in farm implements, and astonished farmer fathers found their children knowing more than they did themselves about the growth of crops, and began to wonder why. One wrote to the headmistress, who showed me the letter. I told her I thought it was better to teach well what I knew, rather than attempt something I wasn't too sure about. But it was a blessing my sister returned to her post quite soon, for I am sure that the school's horse-dealing mistress would soon have got the sack.

As my efforts as a schoolmistress were not too successful, except from the children's point of view, I returned to my horse-dealing, and as summer was approaching I decided to turn to making polo ponies. The manager from the *estancia* where I had been said he was due for his leave shortly and would bring my ten horses home for me. This suited me very well, as otherwise I should have had to send someone out for them, for I was much too bad a sailor to want to fetch them myself. I found that the entire cost of bringing them home would amount to only about twenty-six pounds each, from *estancia* to Oxford, and as I had paid a maximum price of fifty shillings each for them to begin with, they would arrive here at a total cost of under thirty pounds each. I could hardly wait to meet my own favourites again. My little grey Arab Wendy was the one I had missed most – but I have already told you a little about her. She was the one that I had bought from a neighbouring *estancia*, when she was going to be sold as untrainable. She was extremely highly strung, and terror had made her rear up and fall over backwards, a trick which had cost the lives of three men who had tried to break her in. When I had gone to look at this neighbouring *estancia* and the wild horses had been driven in for me, I had found that I couldn't take my eyes off the glorious grey with the proudly arched neck and the long flowing mane and tail. She had snorted as she wheeled madly round the corral at the approach of any human being. I had pointed her out to the foreman, and he had said I couldn't have her, for she'd kill me. I didn't think she would, and directly I saw her I knew she was mine. I loved her wild spirit, and I felt that she had probably been driven to distraction, akin to madness, to kill those men. I had got my own way in the end, and the little grey mare had become mine. She had been more terrified than any horse I had ever come in contact with.

When we first met I stood quite still within about four yards of her, and very gently blew down my nostrils. She advanced and raised her beautiful nose to mine, and her sweet-smelling breath reached my nostrils. At once we belonged to each other for eternity. I saddled her up with infinite gentleness, making no hurried movements, for all animals hate quick-moving people. I slid my hand along her back and down her tail and legs, and she never moved. I mounted her, talking to her all the time in a whisper – for I always talk to my animals in a whisper, or what I call my 'little voice'. It is quite high-pitched, but soft. Dogs adore it. I was riding in a skirt that day, as I always rode in a skirt in summer, a divided one, lined inside with chamois. I found this extremely useful in breaking horses, as it flapped about and got the horses used to flapping things. For a week I rode my beautiful little mare, and she went as the perfect mount should – with effortless paces that made riding seem like floating on a cloud. Then, one day, I couldn't find my old skirt, my maid explaining that the manager had wanted some rag and had said that, as he knew I had got a new skirt from England, I wouldn't mind him using my old one. I was terribly put out, feeling that it was a silly thing to change one's clothes like that, but I mounted Wendy and away we went, and the new skirt didn't seem to worry her. Suddenly she saw something move in the grass – a snake perhaps – and she shied violently; my new skirt shot up and down on her flank, terror gripped her, and up and over backwards we went. Luckily I was ready for her, and, as she went up, I leant round her neck, and as she fell over I was thrown forward not backwards, and was completely unhurt, still holding her reins.

Slowly I got up, as she leapt to her feet snorting and shivering with terror. I stood still and breathed a welcome down my nose; then held out my hand, and she approached me and the fear left her. I knew she was sorry for what she had done, and I knew she had done it on a sudden impulse brought on by fear, and that if I had had my old skirt she would never have done it. She never repeated this performance, and until her dying day remained the most wonderful pony I have ever owned, and that is saying a lot. I feel that one always loves most the animal that causes one most trouble, for it gives one a glorious satisfaction to tame the untameable.

Now to go back. The ponies duly arrived. Some were in a very bad way, having terribly swollen legs from never being able to lie down. I kept Wendy and Judy, two of my own ponies, at home, and the rest went off to stables I had hired, which were a few minutes' ride from the polo ground. I engaged a charming young ex-army groom to see after the ponies. You could see that he loved horses from the way he moved and spoke to them. No harsh words or jabs with a pitchfork from him!

Every day I spent hours training these ponies. It was most exciting to be going to play polo in England for the first time. Wendy and Judy were born polo ponies and I could hardly wait to play them. Two or three of the others were top-class performers too, but it remained to be seen what would happen in a real chukka. It turned out that two or three of the ponies couldn't stand up to the pace of the thoroughbreds against them, so I sold them to army youngsters who wanted safe mounts. But Wendy loved it and nothing could catch her. Judy was as steady as a rock and played without help. I never bothered to use my reins, but simply spoke to my ponies, and they loved the game as much as I did. It was in the middle of a very fast chukka that one of the men fouled, and hit a terrific shot backwards without looking, the ball catching me full in the mouth. I fell forward over Judy's neck with blood pouring from my mouth and everything seeming to be going round and round. Judy had been in full gallop, but as I dropped the reins she stopped automatically and without any help at all walked me quietly to the lines. Someone there took me off and led Judy away. She knew I was hurt and just took me off safely.

I wonder whether people realize how animals know immediately if their owners are hurt, worried, or ill? My own animals always know in a second if anything troubles me.

It was during this summer that I met and married a young doctor. I then sold some of the ponies, and later Wendy was allowed to breed and produced a lovely little filly foal called Windfall.

8   A Farm in a Town

When war broke out my husband was unfit for military service and so was not called up, and we found ourselves in general practice in a small country town. Wendy, and Windfall her daughter, were the only horses I'd been able to keep. There wasn't even a field attached to the house we went to, and no stables. But I couldn't part with either of my ponies, so Wendy made her home in the very big garage, in front of the cars. She could see out of the windows which opened onto fields, and I hoped she would be happy. She was very nervous at first, for being a child of the pampas, she was suffering from living in such an enclosed space, but the doors were left open all day so that she could see us. Windfall lived in the wood-shed: she didn't care where she lived so long as her food came along. She was of a very different temperament from her gentle mother, and I often wondered what her thoroughbred sire's temper was like. She was afraid of nothing, but one often felt she despised all humanity, and when I came to ride her she took much more teaching than most other horses. She knew what to do, but if she thought she could whip round and set off for home she would try to do it. I taught her patiently the folly of her ways, and in the end she learnt to do everything that I wanted, when I rode her without saddle or bridle. I revelled in the way she stopped in a matter of yards from a flying gallop, with her hind feet digging into the ground as brakes. She did it on my word 'sssh', and when she had stopped, she always turned her head round for the piece of sugar she knew she would get. I often wondered, if the sugar hadn't been forthcoming, whether she wouldn't have started off again, and *not* stopped, in order to pay me out. Human beings have very varied temperaments and so have animals, and for that reason it is never safe to say that a certain method of dealing with them will be infallible. Wendy and her daughter were as different from each other as it was possible to be: if Wendy sinned it was through fear; if Windfall sinned it was from lack of righteous fear.

Life in this little manufacturing but countrified town was very different from anything I had ever led before. As wife of one of the local doctors I came under the criticism of everyone, and the people who lived there didn't take kindly to newcomers. I had always been a most friendly person and I was staggered by the way people spoke to us. In the fish shop one morning an old boy said something about his wishing newcomers would stay away, a remark obviously directed at me, so I turned to him and asked him why he was so rude when he didn't even know me. His reply was, 'We always treat foreigners with suspicion 'til we gets to know 'em.' I assured him I was English, but he said, 'You'm a foreigner jus' the same,' and shuffled out. I gathered that it takes at least four years to be accepted as one of themselves.

I found life there rather slow at first and irritating. The perpetual phone calls interrupted my cooking or reading, and people so often seemed to wait until nine or ten o'clock at night before calling my husband out. It seemed unreasonable to me that after a heavy day's work he should have to start all over again, and few nights passed without his having to go out at some time or other. Mostly the calls proved quite unnecessary, but my husband assured me that when night falls people lose their nerve and feel that morning is so far away and that perhaps they should have called in the doctor. He always seemed so placid about everything, but I worried dreadfully over him, for at one time he had had lung trouble. I found the rude way some people rang up and said, 'Send the doctor' instead of

'Would the doctor please call,' or some other polite message, very unpleasant. But I tried hard to remember that they were worried people, for I know so well that we can all be rude and abrupt when we are worried.

But I had many contacts with extremely nice people, and I was deeply touched by the troubles of some of the patients who used to come to call on my husband. Then they would find me sympathetic, and out would come all their worries. I found that if I just listened and let them talk, with just an occasional word of encouragement, it did more good than all the aspirins and brown-coloured medicines that we could produce. I remember once, when my husband was ill and the other doctors in the practice were very busy, I decided to go over to the surgery and run a shuttle service between my husband and the patients for the routine things like renewed prescriptions, only sending over to the other surgery cases that really needed the personal attention of a doctor. One dear old boy turned up and sat down and I asked him what was wrong. He said, 'Nothing new', and that he had just come for a chat with the doctor, but that I'd do instead. So we chatted and I heard his troubles, which were actually more concerned I think with his pigs than with himself. He seemed quite satisfied, and when he next came he told my husband, 'Mrs Woodhouse did me a power of good and I be of a mind I'll come and see her again' – bless him, for words such as those make life happier all round.

One day I was a bit staggered when the telephone rang and a woman's voice demanded that the doctor should go at once to someone who was in terrible pain. I said I was sorry but he was out, and asked if the patient was by any chance having a baby. I got the astonishing reply: 'Don't be absurd, she is a married woman!' Perhaps it was a sign of the times!

I often think one may possess strange gifts, which we

feel certain about, ourselves, though others won't listen to us. The weather is my own speciality. Weeks ahead, if I am concerned in any outdoor function, I know whether or not it is going to rain on the Day. I was on the committee of the local Conservatives some time ago when they were arranging a fête for a definite date in June. I begged them not to arrange it for that day, but to choose practically any other day near it, expecting it to rain heavily on the day they had chosen, but they heeded me not. Nearer the time, I rang up the committee to ask if they'd insured against rain and they said 'Yes', but I was still unhappy. Then there were weeks of sun until the actual day of the fête, when the rain came down in torrents and quite ruined it. The end of the sad story is that the fête committee *had* forgotten the insurance after all, and so lost terribly.

Last year our Coronation committee arranged all their celebrations for Coronation Day, and once again I begged them to hold them on the 6th of June instead, knowing that it would rain on Coronation Day itself. I told everyone about it, so that I could prove I knew it in advance, but again my knowledge was not used. It rained hard, as we all know, and I wondered whether people would listen to me next time.

This gift serves me well in the haymaking season. Weeks ahead I gave instructions for the hay to be cut on a certain day, as I know which days will be fine. Last year I did this as usual knowing that we were going to have only five fine days and that it would rain on the evening of the fifth. But the man came one day late, and I still had two more loads of hay to bring in when the rain came, and those hayloads I lost – but I think I was one of the few who saved any good hay in this district anyway. Perhaps it was the dangers of the Argentine that sharpened this instinct in me, when my life depended on my not getting caught miles from home in a car when it rained torrentially. Anyway this faculty helps me a lot personally, even if so far it has never yet been of any use to the community at large.

Now to get back to our life during the war.

I was greatly worried about the lack of T.T. milk in the town, and I very much wanted to keep a cow, so that I could supply my babies and my husband with the good T.T. milk that they needed. But the difficulty was that I had nowhere to keep a cow if I bought one, for the ponies were already filling the free space in the garage. Finally I went to a builder, who possessed a paddock behind his yard and an old shed in one corner of it. He was a dear old man, and he seemed kindly disposed towards my keeping a cow or two there. Then there was another house with a tiny half-acre of paddock and a stable. So I went and asked if I could rent it for a cow or two, if I bought them. The owner rather liked the idea, if she could buy milk from me, so we came to terms and I decided to rent both places, for I knew that neither by itself would be big enough to keep cows in for long. Next I set about buying a cow. I began by buying a farming paper, and read advertisements that seemed to be full of owners of cattle wishing to dispose of cows of a kind that would be ideal for us. So I wrote to several owners, including one whose description of his T.T. cow warranted its being 'right and straight', with 'money back if not completely satisfied', for thirty-five guineas carriage paid, which seemed too good to be true. He confirmed his offer in writing on delightful notepaper, which with its printed picture of a charming cow gave the future buyer complete confidence. Off went my cheque, and I could hardly await the arrival of my new pet. The station-master told me that it would arrive at six o'clock in the morning so, as I knew it would have had a long journey, I decided to be there and to milk it in the box rather than wait until eight o'clock when it would be unloaded. So, next morning, with new milking stool and bucket in hand I went off to the station in great excitement. I got a sleepy porter to undo the door and I went in – to find a dear little cow quietly waiting there. My heart leapt for joy! I spoke to her, and we breathed a welcome to each other, and I sat down. I started to milk, and it all went straight into my face! Heavens, had I forgotten how to milk after long years without doing so? I changed the angle of my hands, but still I got soaked. It was dark in the box, and I couldn't see what I was doing very well, but I finished milking, although I think more milk had come over me than had gone into the bucket, and couldn't think why. Later, we unloaded her and walked her the few hundred yards to her new home, which was half a mile from our own. She walked quietly and was a pretty little person, but when I got her into her stable and examined her teats I knew that it was not that I had forgotten how to milk, but that it was the nature of the poor beast, for she had a hole half-way up one teat and that was what had caused the milk to come straight into my face. I had been cheated.

We immediately sent for the vet. for, if we had been cheated like this, how were we to know that she had passed the tuberculin test? He injected her to find out, and she failed. It staggered me that anyone, knowing we had small children, could have been so wicked as to sell us such an animal. I wrote a scorching letter to the man who had sold me the cow, and put her back on rail immediately after she had had the tuberculin test. I hated doing this, for she was such a pathetic little pawn in this wicked world. The money came back, but I was five pounds down on her return journey. Years later, when in the man's district, I called on the seller to find out what he was like. He didn't know at first who I was, and I found him a most amusing old chap. Then I felt he must be taught a lesson, and I told him who I was. He seemed to think it was awfully funny and said: 'You'm one of those it didn't work with, others ain't so careful. Come with me,' and he took me into his room, whose wallpaper on examination was seen to consist of a vast collection of summonses. He said that everyone threatened to summons him, but when they came to the point they withdrew, as they didn't want to tell the world they'd been cheated. I guessed I had been lucky to lose only five pounds! I never thought of summonsing him myself, and curiously enough we parted, as boxers part, with a handshake. The old scoundrel had won *that* round!

I tried again. Two cows advertised in Sussex seemed likely ones, so I rang the owner up and told him how I'd just been cheated, and he sounded so very sorry. He offered to send me two cows on approval, if I paid the fare from Sussex, which would be seven pounds. I agreed, and the cows duly arrived. I milked them whilst the cattle-truck waited to take one of them back. They both seemed incredibly difficult to milk, but I supposed that it was my hands that were weak. However, I decided to keep them both, paid the fare, and asked for their T.T. certificates. The reply I got was that they would be sent on, and they came two days later, when I found that the cattle had not come from Sussex at all. Obviously, the man had rung up a friend near me telling him to send me two animals, pretending that they came from him in Sussex. However, beyond having paid the fare from Sussex, when it should have been from only twenty miles away, I seemed not to have lost in any other way, for the cattle were all right. One I found incredibly hard to milk, but a local dairy offered to buy her. So I rang up the man the cattle had really come from and asked him if he had any more? I went over to see him and bought a dear little Guernsey. This man later became just as faithful a friend to me in the cattle world as Bill Organ had been with horses. For years to come I had only to phone him to have perfect cattle sent to me, and our trust was mutual. He, of course, knew nothing about the first deal, when another dealer had rung him up to send me the two cows. But he laughed when I told him about it and said that I had a lot to learn.

I was now producing quite a lot of milk and wanted to sell it; but there were restrictions of all kinds, permits, etc., being needed. In the first place, the sheds I used didn't comply with the Milk and Dairies Acts; but I found the County authorities who dealt with this more than kind and sensible. They could see that I was a trained person and the samples of milk I produced were above reproach. So they gave me two T.T. licences, for the two sheds in different places, and never bothered about air space or drains.

But a very different reply came when I wanted customers. I couldn't get a retail licence, and I had a dreadful fight with the local Food Committee over selling the milk. They wanted me to sell it wholesale to the local dairyman, while I wanted to sell it as T.T. milk to mothers of young babies who needed it. I felt that it would be wicked to mix my beautiful milk with undesignated milk, and said so in no mild terms. I shall never forget facing the committee. I think they intended to have their way, but nevertheless I won in the end.

Every single day in the blackout, summer or winter, I was to be found at five in the morning milking my cows, grooming them, and trying to make them look the most beautiful cows in the district. Their lovely white tails glistened, after they had been washed in soapflakes, for which I could get a permit for washing my cows, although not for washing my babies' napkins! Luckily for the cows, we had only one small daughter at this time, and it had been impressed on her mind at a very early age that it was her bounden duty to dispense with napkins, since the cows needed the soapflakes. As far as I remember, she and our other two babies who joined us later realized that animals were spelt with a capital A in our family, so they all complied without question!

Such is war. I used to leave my customers just as much milk as they asked for – beautiful rich creamy milk, and more and more customers sought me out. Eventually I had five cows, which meant unfortunately that I had now insufficient land for them, and this compelled me to graze them on tiny patches by the railway, or on the assault course at the army depot. No one with twenty yards of grass to spare was safe from my pleadings to let me graze it with my cows. When I moved them from place to place, I put head-collars on them and tied them all to the bumper of the car. They well knew what was happening, for it was thus that we always trekked to new pastures.

Later the army Major, after much pleading and breaking of all regulations, allowed me two unused sheds, which meant two more T.T. licences. Once again the authorities granted my request. I was now selling fifteen gallons a day, and my customers got it at less than the maximum price, for I was doing it as a war effort and not for profit. But that eventually got me into trouble, for a rival heard about it, and I got a warning always to charge the controlled price.

Next rationing came in. I found I had plenty of milk and as always gave people what they wanted, for what was I to do with the surplus milk otherwise? Throw it down the drain? More trouble – so I gave up retailing and now sold my milk to a little private dairyman in the country, who used to come and fetch it daily. Alas, I missed the fun of chatting to my customers.

It was not long after this that disaster befell me. Foot-and-mouth raged, and my cattle caught it. They were not really ill at all, but I knew the symptoms, and it was with a very heavy heart that I phoned the police, for I knew that all my beautiful cows at one of my holdings would have to be slaughtered. I don't think anyone who hasn't owned cows can understand the feelings one has about them. People think of them as rather stupid creatures, that don't know the difference between a milking machine and their calves. But I myself know cows to be extremely affectionate and intelligent animals. Mine were like children to me, and, when I arrived to see after them in the mornings, their beautiful brown eyes looked at me with undisguised love. As I bent down to feed them they often used to bury their damp noses in my hair, just as if they loved the closeness of me. I used to sing to them whilst I milked them, and although I don't claim to be much of a singer they used to listen with a dreamy sort of satisfaction. The milking of them accorded with the tune I was singing. Very often, if I stopped, they would turn round and fix me with a pleading look, just as much as to say 'Go on, do.' If I was not placid, if I was worried or upset, there was always a marked drop in milk production, which certainly seems to suggest that cows are sensitive creatures.

The cowshed itself had a soothing effect on me. The quiet atmosphere and the unhurried calm with which it is necessary to deal with all animals, if you are going to get the best out of them, had that soothing effect on me which is so essential to a happy life. The happy task of combing out their beautiful white tails and grooming their coats until they shone, gave me a tremendous pride of ownership. I used to open the door and let them out to graze, and then just stand there admiring them. Often I was joined by the old owner of the yard I rented. He had retired and found life rather empty, and I think my cows gave him a new interest, dear old chap. Most mornings, in the darkest winter days, he used to come down about six o'clock and watch me milk. The cows never minded him, and we used to revel together in the buckets full of frothy milk that they gave.

One day he told me he came because he never liked the idea of my going out into those dark fields alone, for fear that I should hurt myself. So, at over seventy, he demonstrated that the age of chivalry was not yet past, and he continued to come down just to make certain that all was well. He never struck me as being made of the same sort of stuff as most of the people in that district, and he told me one day that his one ambition was to go to the station, then take his boots off before he got onto the train, so that as he left the district for ever he would not even carry away the mud from it on his boots! Poor old chap, his wish was never fulfilled, and he died where he was born.

I think he was as heartbroken as I was when my cows were slaughtered, for he lost his self-appointed task and we no longer had our friendly morning chats together. He died soon after this and I felt I had indeed lost a friend who loved animals as I did.

When they slaughtered my cows, they left me two that I had down in the army barracks two miles away. These two had not been in contact with the others, so the risk was worth taking. The Ministry paid me far in excess of the value of the cows that I lost, and it seemed to me that they tried to make up to me for the terrible loss of my small herd. I was grateful too that I was allowed to keep my two others, for they could eventually start my herd again.

But there were great difficulties for me in keeping these two animals, for it was against army regulations for cows to be kept there, and awful unexpected inspections always seemed to be coming. One day we were all of us desperate. Brass hats in number were coming, and one of my cows was going to calve on that day almost undoubtedly, which meant that I must be present. Yet how could I be there and not be spotted? And what would the punishment be for the officer in charge, if he were caught allowing cows and a woman on army property?

I arrived there very early in the morning and sure enough the signs and symptoms were obvious to me: she would calve within a few hours. After hasty consultations, the C.O. decided to hide me by erecting a barricade of wood to partition the shed and by putting coal in the front half, and there I was behind this barricade attending to my expectant mother. Every half-hour or so a soldier would come to enquire how things were progressing, for the men were all amused and interested in my cows, and the whole time my cows were in this curious encampment, it was the soldiers who filled their water bowls at night to save me coming the two miles again after I had left them in the afternoon. I always knew that if anything went wrong someone would come and tell me.

Behind my barrier, I heard the noises that indicated the arrival of important people. My little cow was now in heavy labour and I was terrified that she would calve at once and speak a welcome to her new-born within the hearing of the important personage. I heard him approaching and enquiring what was in that shed? The reply was 'Temporary coal store, sir', and the steps came nearer – so did the calf! But just as the new baby came into the world, the noise of steps died away again. Thank heaven I was safe! Some half-hour later my little calf was up and sucking from his mother; the soldiers came and removed the barricade, and all was well. And how helpful they all were! I don't think any of them had ever seen such a very new-born baby, and they all wanted to bring fresh water or fresh straw and to help wash the mother. The C.O., too, came along later just to have a peep. I felt it was rather a wonderful thing that he had risked a severe reprimand just for a cow!

9 Conversation Farm

My belief is that most things that happen to us are ordained for a set purpose, but at the time I could see no purpose at all in most of my cows having foot-and-mouth disease! Some months later, when I was about to have another baby, I had to try to find someone to milk the one cow that I had left to me, so I approached the local War Agricultural Committee, who provided an emergency milking service, and I told them that I should need someone to help me for about three weeks. They asked why this was and I gave them an explanation, and they assured me that they would be delighted to supply a milker when I'd had my baby, but they could not do so until then. Please would I tell them when that would be. I wondered whether anyone ever before had been asked to put into writing the exact date and hour that her future child would be born! It seemed to me quite ridiculous that I should have to continue to milk the cow right up until the last minute. But there it was: my case was not yet an emergency. I was indeed glad that I'd only the one cow left, for I think the five of them would have been too much for me. But I dreaded handing over even my one cow to anybody else to milk, for I felt quite sure that she would go down badly in yield, though as it turned out that didn't actually happen. The evening finally came when my offspring decided to arrive, and I thought it about time to warn the War Agricultural Executive that the emergency was at hand. So I telephoned the office, but only to hear that they hadn't a single girl left, so many farmers being ill or away on holiday at that time. But I replied that they had promised to help me, and asked what I was to do. It seemed that the answer to this question was not written down in the regulations! After all, surely the cow could be brought upstairs if necessary to be milked by me! And that is what actually happened to me once when I was ill as a child and no one could milk my goats. Mother brought a box to my bedside, and one by one my goats came upstairs and I milked them. But a cow is different, even if house trained! My husband thought of a girl in the next village whose employer now bought my milk wholesale, so he left the house to go and see if she would help me in my desperate plight. I knew time was short, if my baby was not to be born in a cowshed, so I got into the car and went down to do my cow three miles away. Somehow or other I got her milked, bedded down, and settled for the night, and three hours later my own new little daughter was born. I felt she was bound to be an animal-lover, born in these circumstances, and so indeed she is.

The milkman's girl came to my rescue, and so all was well. But it was a narrow escape from having to have a cow in my room!

In front of our house was a disused tennis lawn, which badly needed the grass kept down. But we were afraid to let the horses eat it, for our landlord was not in the best of temper, having failed already, much to her annoyance, to insert a clause in our agreement that horses should not be kept in the garage! And we knew that if they were allowed to graze the lawn she would go really mad. So we decided to buy two Chinese geese instead, to keep the grass down, and these geese and I became great friends. Long ago I had had two lovely pet geese in the Argentine, the two who were so unfortunately drowned on our removal 'trek', who used to come and sit on the *patio* with me when I sunbathed there. So it was natural that I should have an affection for geese, having had such happy associations with them before; but these geese were cleverer by far than I had thought possible.

Our new little daughter Judith, for some unexplained reason, cried much as a baby, and I remember having walked with her almost non-stop for seventeen hours. I even went so far as to sling a rug round my shoulders and go for a walk over the fields with her, the rug taking the weight from my arms onto my shoulders. The only time when she was normally quiet was when being driven in the car, so we sometimes jumped at the chance of paying a patient a visit, for it would mean a few minutes' peace. If I were to put her in the pram, it would mean that she would wake every few minutes and would then have to be rocked to and fro. But one morning there was complete silence, and after about an hour and a half I went to find out the reason for this unaccustomed peace. There I found the gander, with his beak firmly fixed onto the arm of the hood, gently rocking the pram! I went to fetch my cook for her to see it, and my camera, but unfortunately in moving house at some time I have lost the snap that I took of the scene. If only a newsreel could have taken it! I suppose he had watched me so often that he had learnt what to do, bless him. After that I had only to put Judith out on the balcony in his charge and I could safely get on with whatever else I wanted to do. Often I have seen him and his wife sitting beside the pram asleep until Judith cried; then immediately the gander got up and took up his self-appointed task. But the goose never did it.

But, sadly enough, tragedy came to my pets once again. We had never thought of foxes in a town, and the geese were allowed to sleep happily in a run with an open shed, but alas, one day when I went into the garden, both had disappeared, and, as it was December 18th, we felt sure that they'd been stolen for someone's Christmas dinner. But no! the police, whom we'd called, found them dead and almost completely buried some distance away in a field. The fox must have come miles for them, and we were heartbroken, blaming ourselves terribly for not having thought of the possibility of a fox in the middle of a town. And, sadly enough, I had not only lost my friends but my self-appointed Nanny as well.

And talking about queer things happening in a town, I don't think the inhabitants of the town where we were then living will soon forget a hayrick being made in our backyard, where normal inhabitants used to hang their washing.

When the geese died, the grass again grew into hay, so we got an old man to cut it with his scythe, and our first hay was made. Then I had an idea: I had often noticed the council authorities cutting the squares and triangles of grass that are so often to be found in a town, and I thought I would ask the council if I could fetch the grass away as they cut it, for I had remarked on what lovely grass it was. My request was duly granted, so I bought a little trailer and fixed it to the car, and collected the grass as it was cut day by day. I used to ring up the gang foreman to find out where they were cutting and then I would go out to pick up the grass. I brought it home to our backyard and there spread it out on the concrete. The children thoroughly enjoyed the fun of turning it, and our rick grew steadily on a small space in the drive, finally leaving very little room to get the cars in and out. My husband used to join in the fun, as he was an expert with the scythe, and anyone nearby who had a patch of grass in their garden that wanted cutting got it cut free of charge and carted away. Soon we were inundated with requests for our services, and during that summer our rick grew to approximately two and a half tons, finally being nicely topped up. I pulled it in the correct manner and shaped it up, and one of the local farmers who was a patient of ours said he thought it such a beautiful rick that he would send his best thatcher to thatch it for us. He kindly supplied the lovely clean straw that was needed, and for two pounds our rick was embellished with all the dainty art of the expert.

People used to stop and stare as they passed, and our animals thrived on our home-made hay in the winter that followed.

When my new little daughter began to mend her ways, I employed a girl to help to look after her and her elder sister, and once more set off myself to buy cows to start up my smallholding again. Someone had told me of a pretty Guernsey heifer in a bunch of shorthorns some miles away, so I went to see it. I found all the cattle there extremely wild, as they had been turned out and left with a young bull. Nobody knew when they were due to calve or anything. But I liked the look of the heifer and bought her, even though I had been able to see her only from some distance away. The farmer promised to deliver her by lunch time next day. But tea-time came and still no heifer. Alas, he was not on the telephone, so I went off to see what had happened. When I got there, I found the whole family out in the field with all the cattle careering madly around. They tried hard to corner my heifer, but she leapt over one fence and other obstacles that she found in her way. At this I begged the farmer to stop chasing the cattle, for fear he would lose the then unborn calves. He asked me how was he then to catch them at all. I said I knew well enough how to catch a horse, and I wondered if my method would work with a heifer. So I asked them all to move away, and then I got as near as I could to my own particular beast, which was in fact not very near. However, I stood quite still and began to blow down my nostrils. The heifer looked at me with surprise in her terrified eyes; then, as I didn't move, she took one step forward, and again a few more, until finally she reached me. Then, up came her nose to mine, and we softly breathed each other a welcome. I stretched out my hand to stroke her heaving flanks and neck, and then caressed her gently behind her horns, which is where cattle like best to be fondled. I asked the men to throw the halter to me; and I put it on, and then, without more ado, she followed me into the waiting truck with no remaining signs of fear. I am sure that the most important thing to watch is that all one's movements should be completely unhurried. One should show no excitement at all, but just appear to take it as all in the day's work. Speak always in a very low voice, using endearing words, for animals love the human voice and its tone means everything to them. The actual words used don't matter a scrap. I can say 'You hateful horrible brute' to a dog, in a loving tone, and its tail will wag furiously all the time; or I can say 'You adorable pet', in a cross tone, and the dog will be miserable.

The heifer proved to be the best possible buy. She soon had a lovely heifer calf and my herd was thus started off again.

About a year later, we felt we simply must have a holiday, since for five years past we had stuck by our animals, without leaving them at all. Then a most exciting possibility presented itself. A patient, who was talking to me one day and listening to my tale of longing, told me she owned a house in a lovely little seaside village in Wales, with lawns stretching right down to the sea, and cliffs nearby belonging to her house, half of which was at present unfurnished. And this unfurnished half she offered us, to our delight, for our holiday. I explained to her that we hadn't taken a holiday for years because of our animals. The horses would have been all right turned out in the cows' paddocks, but unfortunately there must always be someone there to milk the cows, which the girl from the next village, who did sometimes help me in small ways in emergencies, couldn't manage, having cows of her own to do and her milk round to look after. I myself now had five cows and two calves, which would have given her much too much extra work to do. So my friend at once suggested that we should not only take over the half of her house that was unfurnished, but that we should also bring the cows with us, to graze on the cliffs, for there were some old sheds available that I could milk them in. This seemed to us a wonderful idea, but what a job to take cows and furniture, as well as children! However, we quickly made up our minds, and the plan soon materialized. We hired the largest cattle truck in the district, and into that first of all went the barest necessities of furniture, and then the cows; next a solid partition, and lastly the cook and the nursery maid with all the babies' things that they needed. They had two arm-chairs to sit in and seemed most excited about the whole adventure.

The rest of us set off in the car, closely following the lorry, it being agreed beforehand that at a prearranged signal with a white handkerchief the whole cavalcade would stop. And this we did when we reached the Severn ferry, where we were glad to get out of the car to stretch our legs on the boat. Half our journey was done, but the children were already getting a little fractious, Judith being only fifteen months old and Patrick still quite tiny. Soon, however, the fresh air of the river enlivened us all. There was a strong wind blowing, which soaked us with spray, and the ferry was being blown off its course, but all was well, and once on the other side we loaded ourselves into the car again and continued on our way. At long last we reached journey's end, the last mile of the road being down a tortuous winding hill, full of great pot-holes and running water, and on either side high stone walls with tongue-ferns growing in them in profusion. It was almost dark, so thick were the trees and vegetation, and we shivered a little as we imagined the ghosts of smugglers passing by. We had heard that the old house by the sea was reputed to have been a smugglers' hideout – they were supposed to have kept their contraband there in the wonderful underground cellars. The house was square and whitewashed, nestling close to a gigantic cliff. The sands in front came up to the stone wall that surrounded the garden, and when the tide was very high one could jump off the wall straight into the sea. On rough nights the spray would blow right over the windows; and on the beach, as the tide receded, giant caves appeared, offering young explorers hours of fun.

The lorry bumped to a stop at last, the back was let down, and the two girls got stiffly to their feet. We soon unloaded the household luggage, and before very long the tired cows were able to get out. But they seemed quite unperturbed by their journey, and directly they reached their rough shed they lay down and began to chew their cud. Our first thoughts then were of tea. Then we explored the house, which was fascinating with its tiny narrow passages, although they made it very difficult to move even small furniture about the house. The floors were uneven and creaked a little, and the house smelt rather fusty – but what did that matter! We had to put Judith's cot in the passage outside our room, for she was such a light sleeper that she could not sleep with us at all, as even turning over in bed would waken her. Little Patrick was too tiny to bother what happened and slept peacefully in a Moses basket. Our eldest, Pamela, spent her time dashing about wildly with squeaks of delight at everything she saw, and before long she was being taken down into the dark, dank cellars by our hostess's little daughter, who was of the same age. I think she was terrified, although she wouldn't admit it.

With tea over, I sent the children onto the beach with their father to explore, whilst I went out to see after the cows. They looked quite contented, but didn't give much milk that night. This was a relief, for I didn't know what on earth I was going to do with the milk anyway. When I was a bit rested, I intended to go and see the farmer at the top of the hill to ask if he could find room for it in his churn. It seemed a crime to throw it away, when milk was rationed, and the butter that we made in too big a quantity went rancid before we could eat it. Fortunately he agreed to add it to his churns if I promised to keep quiet about it, for everything one did in those days seemed to break regurations of one kind or another.

That first night we went for a glorious walk on the cliffs, with the children safely asleep after their tiring day. It was too heavenly! The wide expanse of sea sweeping in a great curve for as far as the eye could see, and the bracken and the sweet-smelling thyme making one want to throw one's head back and take in great breaths of its goodness. I straightened my tired body and seemed to feel an inch or so taller. We had taken our friends' dog with us for our walk, a charming brown-eyed youngster who never obeyed an order of any kind.

I vowed I'd try to help him mend his ways before my stay ended, and I started on him, in fact, the very next morning, by putting him on a long bit of string and calling him. But he just wagged his tail in a defiant manner, and galloped off. As he neared the end of the cord, I called him again, but he never even bothered to look round. I then gave the cord a terrific jerk, which swung him quickly round until he faced me, and I scolded him. He looked shamefaced and very surprised, so I now changed my voice to a soft welcoming one and called him to me again. At first he wasn't at all sure what to do, because he had been beaten more than once for this running-off trick; but as I continued to encourage him he thought he'd risk it, and he came to me with a curled-up waggly tail and a nervous smile playing on his upper lip. I bent down and stroked his head and scratched his chest, and told him all the loveliest things about himself and his forebears, and this seemed to him splendid. I then tried removing the cord again and away he went, but on my first call he came running back for some more flattery, which I duly lavished upon him. After that he always came to me when I called, although I am afraid his master was not quite so successful.

The average Englishman doesn't really approve of expressing sentiment – that isn't my own feeling, and I always affirm that, although one must speak commands with a firm voice that brooks no disobedience, one should give due praise when the command is obeyed, and in a voice that one usually keeps for one's most precious babies. I think the truth is that I always feel such a surging love for a well-behaved animal that they sense it without fail. I feel that I want to kiss them, and to transmit my love to them through my fingers and through my voice.

Most of our days were spent on the beach, which we greatly enjoyed; but the cows found the cliffs strange and were not too happy for the first day or two. They were used to trees and soft grass, but here they found brambles and bracken, and grass only if they searched for it. At first they were too lazy and well fed to do this, and would wait at the gate between milkings wanting to come in again. But I had to harden my heart, and they at last learnt to go and search for their food. Sometimes their udders got a bit scratched on the brambles, and then the flies would get troublesome, and this in the end compelled me to keep them indoors in the daytime and let them out only at night.

Not long after our arrival Sunrise, one of my best heifers, showed that she was going to calve at the expected time, and she grew restless and stood alone; so I got an old loosebox ready for her and she left the other cows. I peeped at her constantly, and then stayed with her when her time came. People usually say that animals prefer to be alone at these times, but I have never found this to be true. I sit quietly and unmoving in a corner, and I have always found that the animal, whether it be horse, cow or dog, will take an occasional friendly glance at me and seem comforted in its darkest hour. That means that I am always ready to help, if need be, and it keeps me happy, for if I were to leave my cow alone I should keep worrying and coming back constantly to see how things were, and of course that must be much more upsetting for the mother-to-be.

Sunrise calved peacefully in her strange home and in a very short time a lovely heifer calf was bouncing about. I left them together and went back happily to my family.

Daily the little calf used to come on the beach with the children, and race over the stones and the sand castles. The sand on the beach wasn't too good, but she didn't care, and soon her little feet grew hard on the stones, and before long her mother joined the other cows again and forgot her calf. My own experience is that cows fret less if their calves are taken away a few hours after they are born. The cow then seems to transfer its mother-love to me and often turns round and gives me a lick.

It was only a few days after the birth of her calf that the mother appeared to be ailing. I noticed her tail hanging in a bent curved-inwards position which, if you know cows, you recognize as the first sign of something being wrong. When I see this, I bring out my favourite remedy of strychnine and ether, which is a general tonic of a proprietary brand and a strong stimulant. I give it no matter what is wrong with a cow or new-born calf, for it can do little harm and more often than not does much good. When I took her temperature, I found it to be a hundred and three. I then listened to her lungs and knew she had pneumonia. Clearly this was a matter for the vet., but in any case, however much I knew, I hated treating my own animals. I had a feeling myself that she had a piece of wire in her lung, but he thought it was just a chill. The rest of my holiday was spoilt worrying over her, even if I *was* doing for her as much as it was possible to do. Her calf, however, in the meantime, thrived on another cow's milk, and soon she herself slowly got a little better, although she had to be kept in all the time.

We had a wonderful time on our holiday, taking picnics to other coves nearby, and rambling far and wide over the cliffs, but all too soon it came to an end, and back we had to go in the cattle truck just as we had come.

My little cow was still unwell, and didn't seem to pick up at all, and soon after we returned home she died quite suddenly. On a post mortem she was found to have in her lung a piece of wire, which had been partly fibrosed off. It seemed that there was nothing I could have done. She must have eaten a piece of the wire from the old war defences on the cliffs. At any rate, the war damage people thought so and paid up in full; but I had lost my lovely cow, which I felt no money could replace – all I had left was her daughter.

While I am on the subject of sick cows, I want to say how simple it is to give medicines to them, if one doesn't frighten them in doing so. So often I have noticed herdsmen grab fiercely at their cows' noses, and pour the stuff down their throats in a series of rough doses, the animal becoming terrified. I feel that when this happens the risk of some of the medicine being inhaled and thus causing pneumonia is very real. My own method is to get my left arm round under the animal's chin, bring my hand up the other side, and then put two of my fingers into its mouth against the bottom jaw, her head being pushed towards me. Then the medicine goes down in a gentle trickle, giving her plenty of time for taking a breath in between if she wants to. Another way is to place your left arm over the cow's nose and to insert the fingers into her mouth on the far side, away from you, tucking her head round towards you at the same time. I myself never lift the head right up, for it is unnatural and frightening to the animal. My own cows know when they have to take medicine and don't struggle at all, however nasty it is. Old Queenie, my favourite, gives a big cough at the end, to make me think I have choked her with my ministrations, but she always leaves it until too late to convince me I have done her the slightest harm.

When my dogs are ill, we usually take professional advice and then carry out any necessary injections ourselves at a time when the dog is naturally relaxed and sleepy. I feel that these injections, if given by a stranger, may do a lot of harm to a dog's temperament, for they begin to connect a stranger with a nasty prick and thus be frightened permanently by such action. I know most owners cannot manage to do this, but it is different for us, my husband being a doctor, and I myself having done a three-years' course in veterinary science, and we feel we are thus quite capable of doing it for ourselves. One thing I have found, from a long observation of dogs, is how seriously the lack of vitamin A affects big dogs. They tend to become slow in action, and to suffer from minor digestive troubles which make them rather offensive to have in the house, and generally they seem to lack spirit. But one capsule per day of vitamin A, taken for a few weeks, and the dog will be a changed person. He will become bright and quick and ready for anything; his digestion improves, and wild horses won't hold him when there is any suggestion of a walk. I give this to readers for what it is worth.

Not long after our holiday adventure the tension of war seemed easing off and it looked once more as if we could begin again to plan our lives, instead of having them planned for us. We had been looking forward for so long to having our first real home, where we could keep our animals without driving miles to look after them.

My husband and I had quite decided that the life of a general practitioner was not one that either of us had the strength to carry on in peace-time, so he now decided to study to become a specialist. I felt confident that I could keep the family going with my farming, while he completed his studies, if we were able to have a small farm, for there seemed always to be a good demand for fine cattle, and I felt I could buy and sell them successfully as I used to do with horses, and thus help the budget.

One week I advertised two of my young heifers, as I now had too many to keep myself, and they were sold over the telephone within a few hours of the advertisement coming out. After they had been sold, I got another call – from a man's voice on the other end – asking for my heifers. I told him they had gone, but he asked me if I knew of any others, for he wanted to buy about twelve. I told him that I knew of plenty more, for my old friend who had sold me my original two always had plenty to choose from. He then asked me to buy twelve for him and said he would send me a blank cheque with which to pay for them. When I asked him how he knew I wouldn't cheat him and bolt with his money, his simple reply was that he liked my voice! I had no answer to make for the faith that he'd placed in a voice, for of course he must have sensed that I'd do my best for him. But that, strange to tell, was how I started my dealing. I added two pounds to the price of every animal I got for him, and in the end I bought forty cows altogether, for this stranger whom I have never met to this very day. This experience was never quite repeated, and that was the only blank cheque I was ever given; but I have bought dozens of cattle since then for other people I have never seen. Sometimes, years afterwards, I have met them and they have introduced themselves to me, and they have then expected me to remember the animals I had chosen for them in the past.

10   Life on twelve broad Acres

War ended at last, and we were free now to go where we wished. So every week we scanned the farming papers for descriptions of little properties for sale within reasonable reach of London, where my husband would be studying for another three years. One day at length I picked up a paper advertising a smallholding near Aylesbury, with six acres for sale – and more land available to rent – and a small house and plenty of outbuildings. I rang up the owner at once and said I'd be up to see it at twelve o'clock the same day. My husband couldn't get away from his work so I promised to ring him in London after I had seen it.

With a singing heart I raced the car up to see this little place, which I already knew in my heart would be our new home.

It turned out to be a quaint little place that had been converted from two farm cottages and, though not pretty, it was made of old bricks which gave it the charm of age. I felt that it would be very much improved if a garden were made around it. But it was the enormous old barn and stables that really fascinated me. Here at last our animals could have comfort, and even had the house been hopeless I think we should still have bought it, for our animals have nearly always come first in our thoughts – after all, we humans can fend for ourselves! Within twenty minutes the house was ours. I signed on the dotted line, and paid the deposit – and all this without consulting a solicitor about anything. I know now that it was all hopelessly unbusinesslike, but fortunately nothing happened to cause us to regret the transaction.

When I got home to my family I was bubbling over with excitement, and the following Sunday we all went to see it again, and to decide upon our plans. I soon found a good local small builder, and the barns took shape as cow-sheds under my guidance. There seemed to be endless rules that one had to obey in the cowshed world, but I was adamant about one thing: I would not have beastly deep channels running behind my cows at any price, or nasty tubular collars to go round their necks, or drinking bowls they couldn't get their whole faces into if they wished. My own cows were going to have nice wide stalls, gently sloping, and long comfortable chains to go round their necks, so that they could move freely. Then there was to be a wide channel of deep water in front of them, where they could really quench their thirst. Who has ever tried to quench his thirst out of an egg-cup! Well, that is how I regard water bowls for cows, for I have so often noticed the happy way horses and cows dip their noses deeply into water and swish it around, when they are thirsty, before actually drinking their fill. My own cows should have this pleasure, whatever the local authorities might try to do. Fortunately they realized that I had set opinions of my own and that they were helpless to change them, and I soon found them most helpful, so long as I didn't disobey the Milk and Dairies Order too flagrantly. 'What about steriliz-ing and cooling?' they asked. I told them that if the milk were cleanly produced it shouldn't need cooling; that cool-ing was only essential to keep the bugs that were already in the milk from multiplying too rapidly. And I maintained that those particular bacteria wouldn't be found in my milk at all, and that, until they found the milk to be in an unhealthy condition, all I was going to do was to stand it in a tub of water until the dairy called for it. That was all I had ever done before, and I never had a bad sample either there or anywhere else. My sterilizer was home-made: it was a gas copper, with a tin cabinet made to fit over its top, the lid of the copper having been taken away and a hole cut in the cabinet to fit directly over the copper-lid hole. No expensive equipment for me, for with our restricted income we had little money to spare for anything.

Strangely enough, I have always found officials most helpful. I have found that, when they really see that I know my job backwards, they are willing to give me a fair trial – and the amount of red tape that has been cut on my behalf would tie up many less enterprising government departments. In the house for our employees we put in an extra bathroom downstairs, and did a bit of decorating here and there.

The time had now come to give notice to our landlord and to leave the home that we had found it so difficult to put up with. I felt it must have been rather like leaving prison, but the thing that seemed strangest of all to us was the extraordinary attitude of the inhabitants of that unhappy town to our departure. Everyone I met wished us luck and said he longed to be leaving himself for the kind of freedom we were heading for. I felt rather like Moses, and wished I could lead those poor people out of their wilderness. We never understood at all the miserable feeling that persisted in that district. People seemed to live there only to hate it, and yet not to have the willpower to spread their wings and leave it. Often, since we left, we have told strangers about our wartime home, only to see them shudder and then tell us how much they sympathized with us. I wonder if there are many places like that?

It took us about three months to wind up everything, before we could move houses. Even though we had been very unhappy there, we had made many lovable friends and happy acquaintances, and in the end we were very sorry to say goodbye – indeed I had a lump in my throat, when the time came to go, just as I had when finally leaving school after hating every moment of it while I was there.

It took three cattle trucks to move our belongings. Once again our furniture was loaded up, followed this time by our nine cows. Only Wendy now remained of my two horses, for Windfall had been sold when I was too busy to ride. But my poor Wendy was getting very old now, and it wasn't long before I had to take the decision that is so terribly hard for any animal-lover to take – to put her to sleep. When that *has* to happen, I always stay with my pets stroking them, until they have passed on, let us hope, to a place where we may meet again, never to be parted any more.

The animals we have had have always been 'one-man' or 'one-woman' animals. So far in my life three dogs have had the monopoly of my affections and four horses. Other horses I have had by the dozen, and I have loved them all in their several ways, but I never let them become my special loves, knowing that I should have to sell them to make my living. The animals that I have kept for my very own have almost always been ones that I have rescued from ill-treatment or misunderstanding, and have come to me when still suffering fear or even under sentence of death. That, perhaps, is one reason why they have become my special friends and have stayed with me for the rest of their lives. For any animals that I have had to sell, I have always done my best to find good homes, and I have tried afterwards not to worry about them any more, but no other home but mine would have been good enough in my eyes for my own special pets.

Once I had a splendid Alsatian that had been given to me because it was hopelessly nervous. He had one ear up and one ear down, so he wasn't a beauty, but to me he was everything a dog should be, and he never left my side, except when I got very ill with pneumonia and pleurisy, and then he lay anxiously by my bed. Mother had to drag him out for his exercise, and it was on one of these occasions that he was hit by a car, displacing a kidney. The vet. said he would have to be operated on to put the kidney back in place, and, although I was only just out of bed after my illness, I went with him so as to be with him when he was put under the anaesthetic. The operation was successful and I begged the vet. to let me have him back with me, or to let me see him; he insisted, however, that excitement of any kind would be bad for him. I cried bitterly at this, for I knew he would fret for me; but I knew also that if I disobeyed the vet., he would blame me if anything went wrong, so I stayed away. Two days later my Kazan died of a broken heart, and the vet. admitted it – but why won't some people understand that some dogs *will* die, if parted from their owners? It is not stupid to say this, for I am sure that some dogs really do wish to live only *because* of their owners.

After this, it was ten years before I had another dog of my own, and if I met an Alsatian I felt like crying. People will sneer when they read this, no doubt, but if they do that will mean that they have never really loved or been loved by a dog.

I seldom leave my Great Dane Juno now. She loves and tolerates my family, but if I leave her myself, for more than a few hours at a time, she becomes unbelievably miserable. My family understands this, for we are all of us slaves to our animals. And it doesn't seem to us unnatural to feel like this, for immense happiness comes to us *through* our animals, although we certainly have to admit that our lives are to some extent restricted on account of this.

Now let me return to our arrival at our new home. The first obstacle to the move in was the narrow staircase, for it was quite impossible to get our double bed up it, or any other large pieces of furniture. So we summoned the carpenter, cut the bed in half, and then fitted it together again when we had got it into the bedroom. It was wonderful fun getting the little place into order and making it look nice.

The cows were extremely happy in their new home, and it was a joy to see them again in perfect surroundings, in all their natural beauty, with their tails once more all beautifully combed out. Each one of them was now thoroughly washed and groomed morning and night, and I am afraid I used to waste a lot of my time admiring them. One old man once pleased me by remarking: 'I should be quite happy to sleep in your cowshed, Mrs Woodhouse.'

One has to be very proud of one's animals to get the best out of them. I don't mind about their not being 'show' specimens, but their health must always be such that it proclaims itself in their bright eyes and shining coats and alert expression. I can tell sooner than anyone if anything is wrong with them, and this helps me to keep them really fit, for most things can be cured if caught early enough.

It was great fun making a garden for the first time out of a field, and we were lucky to have the expert help of an old retired gardener, the father of the builder who was working for us. At one time he was head gardener to some member of the Rothschild family, and he often looked at me with a shocked face, saying that in those days he never did things in the strange ways that I suggested. He usually did as he intended in the end – and how right he always was! Our tiny plot of kitchen garden grew more vegetables to the square yard than I should ever have thought possible; our pergolas were soon a profusion of roses; and the rockery a sight that would not have disgraced Kew. How happy I was to leave things in his hands!

I soon set about ploughing our twelve acres of land – and little it seemed, to support a family of five, two household helps, and numerous cats and one dog! It was clear that I should have to work it very hard. When I asked the War Agricultural Committee for a daily man, they sent me a German, who hated farm work almost as much as I hated cooking now that there were so many interesting things going on outside. So I taught him to cook, which he enjoyed, and he proved to be an excellent pupil. He soon became so proficient that I was able to hand the cooking job over to him while I took over the farm work myself. I don't know what the authorities would have said, had they known; but I always maintained that it didn't matter who did what, so long as the farm itself got done properly. Eventually, when the German prisoners were released to go home, my Anton returned to his homeland; but he disliked the change so much that he soon came back to me. In the end I had two Germans working for me, who both declared that I worked them harder than they had thought possible, but that, as I slaved *with* them without complaining, they were prepared to put up with it.

My herd grew until I had seventeen cows on the twelve acres. We grew some kale, made our own hay, reseeded all the grass, and were never short of anything except concentrates, which we had to buy. My original cowshed proved to be too small, so Anton and I decided to turn another old wooden shed into a proper cowshed. We forgot, or never knew, that we should have had planning permission or anything else before we made a start, and we had no architect to help us, but I had done building construction and surveying at College, so I was confident that I could teach Anton how to lay concrete, and put in such things as drains – not that he always listened to me, for I remember that parts of the floor had to be torn up again in order to get the fall right. Round the inside walls, after the brickwork was half-way up, we put asbestos sheeting, rendering it properly afterwards for washing down. The floors we scored lightly with a brush before the concrete was dry, so as to produce a nice rough surface that the cows wouldn't slip on; for so many cowsheds look beautiful, but are veritable death-traps for the cows, many losing their unborn calves through slipping down.

We were very proud when the time came to move some of the heifers into their new quarters. One day soon afterwards the milk production officer came to look round the farm, and was much surprised to see the animals so cosily housed. He said he couldn't remember this particular shed being there before, so I kept very quiet, saying only that he must be a very busy man, and asking him how did he like my heifers? Nevertheless, I think he must have suspected that it had only just been built.

Shortly after we arrived at the new farm, I had a letter from the previous county War Agricultural Executive Committee asking me to let them know who had taken over my farm? On the form I wrote 'WHAT FARM?' for I don't think anyone would ever have thought of it as a farm at all, consisting as it did of just one boiler house, one stable, one outhouse, and one army 'coal-store', together with some very small grass-holdings, the largest of which was one acre, and the rest little bits of about a quarter of an acre or less apiece. Nevertheless, all had been reseeded and farmed just as they should be, and our kale crop in the corner of someone else's garden was good enough to have won a prize anywhere, and I certainly did succeed in getting T.T. licences. Everything had been such fun there, fighting against such unequal odds, and that was one of the reasons why this new farm was going to be such an exciting battle, for I had no intention at all of allowing our standard of living to go down while my husband was not earning.

My cattle-dealing in the West of England was now to stand me in good stead, for I found people keen to buy anything that I had to sell, and soon not only was I milking about seven cows, but in addition I had a constantly changing number of visitors awaiting new homes. I would do a hundred miles a day searching for likely cattle, and if I saw a nice-looking heifer in a field I used to stop to hunt for its owner, and it wasn't often that I failed to make a purchase. The heifers I bought gave good yields when they calved down, and the average yield from my own permanent herd was a very high one. I have always milked them all myself – only the shed-cleaning was done for me by someone else – for I am sure that it is the personal attention of the owner, or the absence of it, that makes or mars a herd.

I used also to attend the markets, although I seldom

actually bought from them. But one day in Aylesbury market, as I talked to my husband and waved my hands about as I often do, trying to explain something to him, an amusing thing happened. I had hardly noticed the poor lean old Guernsey in the ring, and certainly had not watched her brought in, although, whilst waiting outside, I had seen her leg bleeding profusely and had spoken to the man who was with her. Nor was I aware of the bidding until a sudden hush, and the words 'Your cow, Mrs Woodhouse', attracted my attention to the cow and then to the auctioneer. I assured him that I hadn't said a word, but he said, 'Oh, I thought you were giving me a signal with your hand,' and I was dismayed at how I had landed myself. I asked how much I had supposedly paid for her, and found that it was thirty-nine pounds. I looked again at the shivering old bag of bones and said I'd take her, for no animal-lover could bear to see the poor old thing suffer any further.

I got her home as quickly as I could and took her temperature. It was so low that it didn't even register on my thermometer, so I got all the old horse rugs I could find and piled them on top of her; then I wrapped her legs in old polo bandages and gave her a hot drink, But she couldn't stop shivering even then, and her poor little calf was none too well either.

The vet., when I sent for him, shook his head and said she had a very bad heart, and he thought she wouldn't live for more than ten days at most. However, he gave me a stimulant for her, and that was all he could do. She had then been calved about ten days and was giving about two gallons a day. By nightfall I had stopped her shivers and her temperature had risen quite a bit, although not yet up to normal. She was now eating well, and was lying down cudding, which is always a cheering sight. I gave her more stimulant last thing at night and she then looked very bright, with her four rugs on. On the following morning she ate ravenously, her temperature now being normal, and

Junia and our kittens

*Untrained dogs after six hours training
on a weekend course*

Patrick, Judith and Chica, Queenie and Snow Queen,
Juno and I await Master's return home

The Author at home with her pets

Aubretia gets a Kiss

Reared in the hot cupboard, he thought he was human

Junia and the baby chickens

Nanny takes care of Queenie's twins;
Patrick and Juno help

her yield about a gallon and a half. Her calf scoured terribly and I had a difficult fight for her life, but daily my old Queenie thrived and her yield rose.

It was enormously exciting, and, at the end of a fortnight, she was already giving five gallons a day, her coat had become sleek, and she was rapidly coming to look like one of my own cows. I never left her without rugs, though she had them off for half an hour, morning and evening, to lick herself and do her toilet. It is quite essential to do this if a cow wears rugs, for otherwise the coat gets rough and dirty.

I soon began to wonder whether my other cows wouldn't do better with rugs on. So out came all my old horse rugs, and the cows all seemed to wonder what on earth I was doing putting these things on them, though they accepted it all without demur, as for the best. Almost immediately, without my increasing their food, their yields rose considerably. So it wasn't long before every cow in my herd had a rug on it, and with it every yield rose, and in not a single instance did I increase their rations. For a whole year I tried this out: in winter they wore thick rugs with waterproof covers made out of ground sheets, and in summer cotton sheets that I had made for them to keep the flies off. It was quite a work putting these rugs on and taking them off, and changing the number worn according to the weather, but my rising milk cheque was good witness of its being worth while.

When Queenie calved again, her condition was magnificent, and she started off with the enormous yield of seven and a half gallons a day. My success with my cows now prompted me to write a letter to farming papers reporting what I had discovered about the rugging of cows, and how I found that they doubled their yields – and that with giving them only half the normal amount of concentrates for the amount of milk produced. This innocent letter brought a veritable hive of people down to my farm. Many of the national newspapers sent reporters to find out what it was all about; Pathé Newsreel made a short film about my work; I appeared on T.V.; and people came from the United States and other foreign countries to hear what I had to say. Fortunately, I was able to substantiate all my statements with official milk records, and I felt quite confident that any farmer who bothered to try out what I was doing would find that what I said was true. Sir Henry Twyford, a former Lord Mayor of London, who was then just starting a Guernsey herd, was one of those who were very keen to try out my method.

The reason for the increase in milk, and the improved bodily condition of rugged cattle, is of course the conservation of heat which makes available extra energy for milk or meat production. It is amazing to see how quickly a rugged cow will put on body weight and increase her yield without extra food. One interesting point is that warble flies cannot complete their life cycle with a rugged cow, because the larvae that normally make a breathing hole in the skin of the back, before emerging to complete their cycle, cannot breathe freely under a rug, and they die. I never have to dress rugged cows with a warble dressing as the grubs are already dead when they are still quite tiny.

As a result of all this publicity, a London firm offered to make rugs to my own design, and I had great fun when they sent down their mobile van complete with seamstress. Their tailor cut out the patterns, after measuring the cows, and some beautifully fitting rugs were made. During the war this firm, John Edgintons, had made covers for aeroplanes and for every other sort of peculiar objects, so coats for cows came just in their stride.

Several other people had rugs made for their cows, and their yields also rose considerably; but one herdsman found it tempting to increase the amount of food as the yield rose, in spite of my strict advice to the contrary. For in my opinion it is not necessary to do that – indeed, I think it quite harmful, and possibly dangerous – for an overfed cow wearing rugs can quite easily get acetonaemia. One man wrote to say that his cows got lice after wearing the rugs for six months, and lost their hair! Stupid man, he had put rugs on and never taken them off, or made certain that his cows were free from lice – if the cows are dusted with D.D.T., lice are never heard of anyway. I have used rugs for my own cows for six years now, and my experience has proved that all the effects are good, though some farmers find it all too much trouble. Rugging cows, however, is nothing new: it was, and still is, unusual in England, but it is often done abroad.

After the publicity I had over the rugging of my cows, I had stacks of letters from people wanting to buy Guernseys, and one man came and offered me a thousand pounds for the new daughter of my old Queenie, which I refused, for I had no intention of selling *any* of Queenie's daughters. It came about, as it happened, that when this calf grew up she played a leading part in a film with Douglas Fairbanks, Jr.

I had one great trouble in the cowshed – rats. Unfortunately the original old cowshed was full of holes and nooks and crannies suitable for the rats to breed in. One evening when I had little Judith with me to see the cows, I put on the lights and found rats there by the dozen. One of them, dazzled by the light, jumped onto my foot and sat there, cool as a cucumber. I cannot stand rats, but I didn't want to show fear in front of Judith, who looked at it with obvious pleasure and said, 'Lovely bunny, Mummy'! But, thank heaven, the creature soon scampered off to its hole. The pest officer had a most strenuous time trying to rid the farm of them for me.

It was about this time that I began to feel that I must ride again, and I wanted the children to learn to ride too. So we bought two little ponies, which the children and I used to ride in turn. It was great fun teaching them to ride, but once on a pony again I found the old urge coming over me to break in another horse, so I went off to a sale at Reading. There I saw a bunch of unbroken Irish horses, and among them a grey filly that reminded me of Wendy. Her owner said she was quite unbroken, but I wanted her terribly, and I succeeded in bargaining him down to twenty-five pounds. I began by breathing up her nose, which made the dealer snigger at me, but it helped me to load her quietly into a box, and she came home and settled down quite cheerfully. Next morning the vet. arrived to do a routine tuberculin test on the herd, and admired my new horse which he saw looking out of her stable. I told him she was unbroken, but that I was just going to take her out. 'Surely you are not going out on the road with all the traffic?' said the vet. But I replied that I was, for the mare wouldn't now do anything wrong.

I breathed a friendly welcome up her nose, gently put the saddle on her back, whispering loving words to her all the time, then pulled the girths up slightly until they just touched her body, knowing that they would be cold which is a thing no horse likes, and having given them a little time to warm up I tightened them until I knew that they were safe. I then gave her a gentle caress with my fingers down under her mane, which all horses love, and I mounted her. At first she just stood still, not knowing what to do; so I leant forward and helped her by pulling a little on her head-collar, and she took a step forward in the right direction. I kept on talking to her, and put my heels against her ribs, pressing her forward and persuading her to move off. In a minute or two she understood, I waved to my family, and off we went for our first ride together.

At first, she was very uncomfortable; although completely safe, she was quite uncollected, which was of course natural. I urged her into a canter, when we reached some grass, and she lolloped along. Then I said 'ssh', and pulled her up. I continued this stopping and starting, and walking round the lanes, for about half an hour, and she did nothing evil. After I got home I felt that I had better teach this mare to wear a bit from the start, for this was England, and not the pampas. So I put a vulcanized pelham in her mouth, attached her reins to it, and fastened it back to the saddle, so that if she bent her head to it in the very slightest degree she would then be on a loose rein. I then left her to chew it, and walk about with it in the stable, for half an hour.

Next I taught her, on the slightest pressure of the bit, to bend her neck and walk backwards, pushing her back by her nose meanwhile to help, always giving the command 'Walk back'. That ended her lessons for the first day, and on the next day we started off with quite a lot of knowledge behind us for she now knew the words to stop and to walk back, and she knew that the pressure of my heels meant 'go on'. Next she had to learn, by neck reining, to turn to the right and to the left. Soon I taught her this by bending over her neck and catching hold of her noseband and thus pulling her round, whilst still laying the reins on her neck in the fashion she must learn to obey. I found she would bend quite nicely to the lightest touch of the reins on her mouth, so she had now become a much more comfortable ride. My voice now took precedence over everything, and she was beginning to know my commands. I took her out twelve times in all, and after that she was the loveliest creature to ride. She would break directly from a walk to a canter, and once in a canter one could hardly feel the motion of it at all. I still held my reins in one hand held chest high, in the way they do in the Argentine, and there was no hard contact of any kind with her mouth. I have often in the past ridden my horses on reins of cotton to prove to people that reins are really quite unnecessary with a well-trained horse.

I was coming home after my twelfth ride, when a large car drew up and signalled me to stop. The driver said he couldn't take his eyes off my pony, and asked me to sell her to him for his son. I told him I had possessed her for less than a fortnight and that she still had much to learn. But in spite of that, he bid me a very large sum for her which, most reluctantly, I knew I ought to accept. I found out later that he was a farmer in a big way, so I knew that she would have the best of everything – but how I had longed to keep her for myself! What a horrid nuisance it is having to earn one's living.

I took her over myself to her new home and saw the boy mount her. He rode in the usual English style, of which I so strongly disapprove, and he never once spoke to her in the voice I had told him to use. He had far too much hold on her mouth, so I told him to let her head go completely free. The reply I got was that 'she must go into her bit' – but what a stupid idea that is, because how needlessly tiring it must be to ride a horse long distances with a weight on the end of the reins, with the hands held down on the horse's withers and the reins in two hands. In his riding there was no evidence of the perfect rhythm one attains by always sitting down to all the horse's paces. But he was fond of horses, and I knew that she would be as kindly treated as they knew how. Yet I vowed that that would be the last horse I would break for an English rider; and I have kept to my vow, for I have no intention that any horse broken to my voice should be subjected to the hands of someone who may prefer rosettes in a show ring to the true understanding of a horse's mind and intelligence.

Only once since then have I had anything further to do with horses, which was when I wanted to buy one for my elder daughter to ride. A lovely half-Arab chestnut was brought to me as suitable for her, and I fell for it, but, when I got on it to try it out, I found it sheer purgatory to ride, having a one-sided mouth as hard as iron and a completely unbalanced movement, and no understanding of words whatsoever. I wouldn't in any circumstances have allowed my daughter to ride it even if it had been given to me. So I bought her another, and decided to rebreak the Arab before passing it on to someone else, for we couldn't afford to keep both of them.

The first day, when I had mounted her and taken her onto the common, she tried a trick on me that clearly she had learnt in the past that would neatly unseat her rider. She swung round and round in close circles until we were both completely giddy, and then fell down; after which she proceeded to try and roll on me on the ground. I took her bit off and put the reins on her head-collar, for it was a bit that had taught her this trick – or vice as I considered it – and a head-collar would break her of it. I mounted again, and again she tried it, but this time she found that it didn't work, for with a head-collar on I could turn her head. So she gave that trick up and I fondled her, continuing down a lane until we came to some trees. Here she tried out another trick she had learnt, that of rubbing her rider's legs against a tree until she was pushed off. Once again the head-collar defeated her; but I was finding this constant battle extremely tiring, so I took her to a big open field to put her through her paces, teaching her by my voice only, to go and to stop. Eventually I put the bit into her mouth again, and rode her on a loose rein. But by now she understood every word of command, so it didn't matter any more what she had on. It took me about eight weeks to make her into a properly trained pony, but I was then able with complete confidence to sell her to one of my near neighbours for their little boy, and since then she has won many prizes in the show ring. But give me a completely untouched horse, that has only fear and not vice to break, for I simply hate the discomfort of a badly broken horse.

Talking of vice, I met my match with a mad cow not long after this. She had come to me a few days before calving, and had then seemed a nice quiet creature. Unfortunately she calved in the field, and when I tried to get her in, she went mad, or 'calf proud' as the dealers call it. This is not just fear, and no friendly breathing would stop this kind of wickedness. She just lowered her head and came to me at a pace which Spanish bullfighters would have welcomed. However, I managed to step aside just in time. I had never met a cow like this before, although I have heard since then that it is quite a common complaint.

It was terribly cold at the time, and foggy, and I feared that the baby calf might catch a chill, so I asked my husband to walk down outside the fence – a completely safe fence she couldn't get through – and I hoped she would dash along after him and that I could then grab the calf. But no, she turned back after me like lightning, although she had at first gone after him. I wondered whether I would try riding the children's pony to drive her in, as the pony had been in the field with her all the time and she hadn't molested it in any way. So I saddled it up and went out to her; but she scented me at once and raced at us, hitting the pony broadside on and sending us flying, before dashing back to her calf. In the fall I broke my arm, and the pony galloped off. Eventually, the little calf fell into the ditch near where my husband stood. So I myself went further up the fence, hoping the cow would follow me – since her one thought appeared to be to kill me if she could – and she raced after me, enabling my husband in the meantime to grab the calf and pull it over the fence. We quickly slipped round and into a shed that led into the field. It was divided into two, so we put the calf on one side of the partition, which was about four feet high, and as the cow came racing in to the other side, I slipped a rope over her head and tied her up. We took the calf away at once, and within a few hours the cow was her quiet old self again. How I ever succeeded in *milking* my cows, including the wild one, with a broken arm, I really don't know! But I have always had to milk my cows myself, however ill I have been, not being one who believes in machines, and somehow I managed it. Using machines, alas, one hasn't the lovely contact with the animals that one has when milking by hand.

The pony, incidentally, was quite unharmed by his encounter with the cow, and that was the first and only cow to behave with me like that, although since then I have heard many stories of a similar kind.

11 A real Farm at last

After living three years on our little farm the time came for us to make another move, for my husband, who had now finished with examinations and had a post in London, found the long daily train journey much too tiring. So we thought once more of finding a house nearer London – a very difficult task, as we soon discovered, for we had to have land and sheds for my cows. However, one day at long last, we saw advertised in *Country Life* a large house with ten acres and stables to go with it. It looked very beautiful in the photograph, but much too large. However, the next day being Saturday, we decided to go over and just have a peep at it. One look was enough: it was certainly old and beautiful, but in shocking repair, and the sheds would do only as temporary quarters for cows. Clearly we should have to put up some new buildings if we bought the property, and it was going to cost a lot of money to put everything in order, but we both wanted it badly. I couldn't get into touch with the agents, as it was Saturday afternoon, so I rang them up early on Monday morning, only to hear that a Country Club had offered to buy it on the very Saturday morning that we had made our own visit. We thought it would be a wicked shame, if a beautiful house like that became a raucous Country Club, so I rang up the agents again and offered them more than the advertised price. I already felt that this house somehow belonged to us, and I vividly imagined our children playing hide-and-seek in its many cupboards and passages. What happened was that our offer was accepted at once, and the place was ours. We then had to find a buyer for our little farm. But that didn't take long; we put it into an agent's hands and sold it within a few days for exactly what we had paid for our new house. So my work with Anton had not been in vain, for the farm fetched four thousand pounds more than we had paid for it.

We now made hasty building plans for cowsheds at our new home and once more there was all the usual red tape to be dealt with; but, as happened to me before, everyone proved to be most helpful. So many were the new precedents, however, that I set up in the building of my cowsheds that some of the officials must I think have feared a little for their jobs. For me, on the other hand, it was indeed exciting to see my range of new buildings going up entirely to my own design. The poor builders who were working for us had less time for their cups of tea than they had ever had in their lives! For if they slacked they found that I myself could lay bricks faster than they ever did and that I knew very well such things as exactly what the concrete mixture should be – in fact, I must have been a hateful person to work for, although my buildings were quite lovely when they were finished. The theme was to be the comfort of the cows – not the saving of my labour – for comfortable cows give much more milk, and I was determined to have records that would beat other people's. Indeed, I wanted my rugged cows to be famous.

While the sheds were being built, we kept the cows in the old stables and in a converted barn, which was very close quarters. We had brought with us seven cows and a bull, and we were now selling thirty gallons a day as well as providing enough for our own household. With one of my cows, the year before, I had made an experiment: for her first calving she was given a rug, and in a period of 317 days she gave 1,010 gallons. For the next lactation we tried leaving off her rugs, although otherwise she had exactly the same treatment as before: this time she gave 645¼ gallons in 321 days – a longer lactation but much less milk. After that she remained rugged as long as we kept her, during her next lactation giving 1,231 gallons in 303 days, then 1,274 gallons in 274 days, 1,102 gallons in 250 days, and after that never less than 1,000 gallons a year until I finally had to put her to sleep. Performances of this kind became a commonplace in my herd: time and time again I proved that rugs were the answer to more milk at lower cost, and I shall never understand why more farmers don't now use them.

At last my new buildings were ready, and it was a thrilling moment when I moved all my animals over. There, now, were my glorious cows all in a row, showing off their beautiful golden colour to perfection against the white walls, while the bull proudly surveyed the world from his own pen. When his wives were out, he could see them from there, even if he wasn't actually with them. And my bulls were always so quiet that my little son, Patrick, would come down to the field with me and ride them. Or sometimes he would ride up one of the cows, sitting on whichever one he fancied and brandishing a small twig – Roy Rogers, at least, in his imagination! We had one very favourite cow called Sandfield Moss Rose, or Mossie for short, who used to lie in the field until the children climbed on her back, and she would then get up quietly and take them for a walk round the field. When they tired, they would slip off, and she would lie down again contentedly.

My cows thrived in their new quarters, and when people came to buy their offspring they were most impressed by the cleanliness of the place and the beauty of the cows. But they were not pedigree cows, but usually other people's low-yielding animals, that I bought partly for the fun of putting rugs on them to prove that they could be turned into valuable cattle. At this time Guernseys were fetching enormous prices, and even my non-pedigree in-calf heifers would fetch two hundred pounds each without much effort, and there was always a good demand for them.

Soon I managed to rent another six acres of land nearby

and was fortunate to be able to buy twelve acres more. It was fun growing corn for the first time, and I tried growing carrots – but I found carrots rather a headache. The land around had been derelict for years, and when it was ploughed you soon couldn't see the land for the weeds. At first I tried cutting them with our little Rotoscythe; but I found that it got too hot, for this was not the sort of job it had been designed for, although it certainly did magnificent work. So the charlock grew thick and high, and in the end we had to get gangs of men to pull it by hand. Many of them got a rash from doing it, but we won eventually and a good crop of carrots was harvested in the end.

The corn I sold as a growing crop, as I had no use for it. I felt now that for the first time in my life I was really farming and, even if it was only twenty-five acres, it was the biggest acreage I'd ever had, and my herd had now grown to nineteen head of cattle including two bulls. But I was nearly killing myself with overworking. Many a time I sat up at night in the freezing cold, while a cow had her calf, and once it was a blessing that I had done so, or I might well have lost our old Queenie. She had been in labour one night for a long time, and I thought she was going to have twins. So at about midnight I decided to call in the vet., who was a stranger to me. He examined the cow and told me not to worry but to go back to bed. It was not twins, he said, and the calf was coming normally, although the cow was not yet ready to deliver herself. He went away, and I didn't go to bed, for I had calved Queenie five times before and this was the first time she had behaved like this. I had never myself examined a cow internally before, and always had got a vet. to do this in case of trouble, but I now decided to find out for myself what was wrong. I discovered that she was actually going to have twins, and that one was coming backwards. There was no time now to send for the vet. again, or even to get my husband to help me, for I knew how serious was the danger of suffocation when calves were born in this way.

Within a few minutes I had delivered bull calf number one, and not long afterwards his sister came to join him – two enormous calves they were! It was the coldest night of the year, so one at a time I carried them indoors and put them by the fire. Queenie herself showed no interest in them, for she was heading for milk fever, so next day the calves remained by our fire, as you can see. We were now fighting for Queenie's life. She had gone down with the dreaded milk fever, and it took three days of injections to get her back on her feet again. It is said that in the case of twins, when a bull and a heifer are born, the heifer is likely to be barren. But these calves being born with separate placentas, I decided to rear them both and to see for myself if the heifer would breed, for it was my own opinion that she would.

All these experiences of mine show how necessary it is for anyone with a herd of cattle, or other animals, really to know the signs and symptoms of ill-health peculiar to their own stock. On the occasion I have described, had I gone back to bed as was suggested, I should most certainly have lost my calves. It is experience that counts, and I often feel that in the veterinary profession the young recruits to this vocation should not waste their time in colleges and assisting only in surgeries, but should be sent out onto the farms to people like ourselves who work personally with our animals.

For many years, when I lived near Oxford, I used to treat most of the sick animals in the neighbourhood when people didn't seem quite to know what was wrong. And here I am now rung up constantly to see if I can help desperate owners who want to save their dogs or their cats. But a law has now been passed which makes it illegal to give advice unless one is on a register of non-qualified practitioners so I daren't help people any more, for fear of getting into trouble through one person telling another – for, if one cures an animal that has been thought to be incurable, the delighted owner will be sure to spread the good news. All this seems to me rather sad.

I remember once, some years ago, going to a farm to buy a cow and seeing in the yard there a lorry that was waiting to load an animal for the slaughter-house, an animal that had been given up as quite hopeless on account of its having some foreign body inside. I asked the man to let me look at it, and I listened very carefully to the sound of its breathing, feeling almost certain that there was no foreign body in the lung. I asked the man to give me three days to cure this cow since she was such a valuable one, and I said that I should be very surprised if I failed. He agreed to do this, so I rugged her up and treated her in my own way. Down came her temperature very soon, she began to eat again, and at the end of three days it was quite obvious that I was winning. The cow recovered completely and eventually became one of Leslie Weston's best cows at Manor Farm, Stoke Mandeville. She may well be in his herd still, for she was still with him two years after I cured her. It seems such an appalling waste of valuable animals that this sort of thing, that I prevented on this occasion, should ever be allowed to happen.

I once lost a lovely cow myself through wrong diagnosis, and there had been nothing I could do to prevent it; for the animal was insured, and the insurance company wouldn't listen to me when I rang them up and told them that my cow would die, if the treatment that was being given was continued, and asked them to let me stop it and treat the cow myself. They refused absolutely, saying that, if I did not do what the vet. said, they would not pay if the cow died. This was a cow worth about a hundred and fifty pounds, and I was too badly off to risk it. She died all right, and on post mortem examination my own diagnosis was proved to have been correct, so I gave up insuring after that.

Some of my knowledge with animals few people will believe. I can tell, for instance, ten days after she has been mated, whether a cow has become in calf to her service. To me the feel of her udder changes, owing I think to the hormone content in the body. She becomes easier to milk, and my fingers, which have grown sensitive, know this immediately. Knowledge of this kind helps me a lot in herd management, but it is a gift that I cannot pass on. Another thing I usually know is what sex my calves have when they are on the way. I know it from the way they lie, and I have been bold enough sometimes to tell other people about their own cows, although I don't much like doing this for fear of disappointing them. Often, in a difficult calving case, I had told the vet. to hurry in order to save my 'heifer' calf. It seems to him queer that I should know, but he usually finds that I am right.

I sincerely hope that this doesn't sound too much like boasting. It certainly isn't meant to be, but I do want to persuade readers that some of us, who spend so much of our time among animals, get special senses given to us, so that we are inclined to brook no argument when we say that we 'know'. The saddest thing for me is that I was never trained as a vet. and in consequence I have to let other people do what I would so much like to do myself. Two years ago I lost my beloved Mossie, because no one would operate on her when I knew she had a foreign body in her rumen. She was moribund next morning, and I put her down to save her suffering. The staple that was killing her had pierced her rumen. Why it is that cattle constantly eat such things I can't imagine. Horses certainly never seem to behave in this way.

After we had been living here about two years, I went shopping one day and among my intended purchases was some tinned soup. My second sight told me suddenly not to buy a certain brand, and I told the grocer this and he wrote down another. But, as things turned out, the wrong soup got sent to me and, when I opened the box of groceries, I put it on one side to send it back. Fate, however, was not on my side, for one of my household, instead of going to the store cupboard for the children's soup, picked up this tin, and prepared it for their supper. Within two hours both my children were violently sick and ill, and the first question I asked was what they had had for supper, and the reply of course was that wrong soup. I raced downstairs to see if I could find the tin, but it was already in the rubbish bin, and I couldn't easily find out what was wrong with it. Little Patrick was nearly well again next day, as he had not drunk much of it, but Judith still had a temperature and was very ill; so I sent for our local doctor, and he and my husband racked their brains to find out what was wrong. She had become paralysed in one leg, but it was quite definitely not infantile paralysis.

Every sort of cure was tried for three months, until eventually she went to hospital where they diagnosed a rare foreign disease and the cure began. In less than a fortnight the paralysis left her, but she remained very weak.

It had been just before Judith fell ill that we bought a lovely five-year-old Great Dane bitch, Jyntee, who inspired my next venture – but *she* must have a chapter to herself.

12 Jyntee and Juno
—Career Dogs

Our Great Dane, rescued from a London suburb in which she had little scope and little happiness, was certainly no show beauty owing to a broken tail received at birth, but to me she was the most wonderful person, highly intelligent and very beautiful. She never left my side and became human in her sympathy, suffering terribly whilst Judith was ill, knowing that something was wrong but not knowing what. When Judith came home from the hospital, she had to stay in bed for some time while she was slowly getting well again, and I spent large sums buying her books and magazines to amuse her. Suddenly I had the urge to write a book for her myself – I would write the true story of 'Jyntee, the Tale of a Dog with a Broken Tail', so I bought a big drawing-book and wrote the story down during one lunch hour. I then asked a photographic agency to send me a cameraman, for I thought we would illustrate the book with real photographs for Judith to look at. By this time she was up for a few hours every day, so she posed for some of them herself, and at last the whole thing was finished.

I read it to her and to many other children, and, as they all seemed to enjoy it, I wondered how I could get it printed. I never thought of submitting my story to a publisher, thinking I would try to sell the book myself, and my next-door neighbour, being a publisher of a magazine himself, gave me the address of his own printers, a small firm that had never done this sort of work before. That didn't worry me, so I asked them to let me have an estimate for producing it, and I thought I would show my drawing-book meanwhile to some booksellers to see if they would buy some if I printed it; and the first shop I went to was in my old home town of Oxford. I am afraid it never occurred to me that it was a silly thing to do to ask a bookshop to say whether they would buy something even before it was finished, but perhaps some kind fairy looks after fools, so in I went. I saw the book-buyer and showed him my book in rough, and he asked me how I was going to bind it, etc. I told him everything I could about it, and imagine the thrill I had when he got his order book out and wrote 'Please supply six "Jyntee" on publication'. I realize now that he must have been the kindest of men to give me this encouragement. I then took it to a big London store and they said that, if it looked as nice when I'd published it as it did in the drawing-books, they would order a hundred copies. I tried one more head buyer of a multiple firm, but here I met my Waterloo, for I was told very firmly that nobody who published a book privately ever succeeded in selling it, and that his own firm wouldn't undertake to buy a single copy if I published it. That just about decided me: I would publish the book if it was the last thing I ever did! For I have never liked the word 'can't'! I felt now that I could hardly wait to get back to Watford to tell my printers that I would borrow the six hundred and fifty pounds necessary to pay for the production, and that I would get a mock copy ready immediately.

Judith's health now improved daily, and she was soon quite well again, and I could concentrate on my book. The poor printers had never been so pushed before. I have never been a patient person, and I expected it to be ready in about a month, which was giving them far too little time for the job they had to do. In the meantime, armed with another mock copy, I set out to learn this business of selling my book. I found that in between milking my cows, and taking and fetching my small children to and from school, I could cover a maximum of two hundred and eighty miles in a day visiting bookshops. But I soon found that book-buyers are difficult birds to catch. The number of times I heard such exasperating phrases as 'The buyer is away today', or 'Gone to the dentist', or 'We don't see travellers today', or 'We are too busy to see you today' – just as if I wasn't busy too! I suppose the polite traveller gives a wan smile and goes on his way, cursing the waste of time and petrol that took him to that particular shop.

But it was one of the greatest thrills of my life when a book-buyer once looked up and smiled and said how lovely it was. But I didn't always get much encouragement, and one shop in Bristol just said 'No, thank you', without even looking at it, adding the remark they 'only bought children's books, not art books', but I felt too annoyed to tell him that it *was* in fact a children's book. Then two shops turned my book down saying that they wouldn't be able to sell a copy of it – yet both subsequently ordered it on publication, which seemed odd to me.

By this time I was getting a bit worried about the actual production of the book, for I had promised my future customers that it would be ready well in time for the Christmas trade. So I spent hours hanging round the printers, spurring them on to greater and faster efforts, as I knew already from talking to people that it often takes approximately a year to publish a book, yet here was I, ignoring the paper shortage and labour troubles and expecting my book to be ready within six weeks!

But the time arrived at last when I watched it go on the giant machines, and then the blow fell. I had discarded so many printed sheets as not being up to my standard – my standard being perfection – that we had run short of paper! Here we were six reams short. In my ignorance, when I heard the bad news, I wasn't too despondent, thinking that surely we could buy such a small amount as that, especially when I knew we had more on order from the mill. But the delay made me irritable, so I set off myself to buy the six reams of art paper that we still needed, of the weight of double royal 100 lbs.

That will be double dutch to those who don't know the paper trade, but to those who did know it in those days of scarcity, it will have seemed a pathetic task that I had set myself. Didn't I know that the paper was available only for export? Or for the programmes for the Festival of Britain? I must have tried nearly every paper merchant in Britain without success, and my book seemed doomed to wait until the next allocation of paper came in, which would mean that my promise to the booksellers that my book would be in the shops for the Christmas trade would not be kept.

I am not in the habit of breaking promises, so I went to many more paper mills, and one finally let me have a few reams off a roll that should have gone for export. I needed so little now to finish my book that in desperation I telephoned a firm of publishers I had heard of and, telling them of my plight, asked them boldly if they'd lend me the few reams of paper that I needed until my new allocation came in. The answer came back at once: 'Certainly you shall have it if we have it ourselves. We'll have a look round and will put it on rail tonight if we can find it.' I don't think I have ever heard kinder words. They didn't know me from Adam and yet without references they were going to lend me approximately sixty pounds' worth of paper! I soon received a telegram to say it had left Scotland and I went to Euston station to get it personally.

But the train arrived without the paper – and I don't think Euston station will ever forget my paper, for I kept them on their telephone for two and a half hours trying to trace its whereabouts! At last we found that it had been shoved into a truck in a siding somewhere in the Midlands and forgotten. I told them I would take my car as far as Bletchley, if they would stop the train for me and take it off, and I think I must have sounded like someone very important for the boat train was stopped, whilst my slow train was allowed to pull into Bletchley, and two porters and the stationmaster came to take off my paper. So there it was at last and the machines rolled on again, and six weeks later I returned the borrowed paper, most gratefully, to the benefactors whom I had never seen.

The book was ready now except for binding. A London firm had promised to do this, but willing binders were then few and far between and although they knew my publication date they didn't care twopence whether I got the books in time or not. They delivered a first supply of five hundred copies and then stuck, and I spent the next week sitting on their doorstep alternating between imploring them to bind the rest and threatening them if they didn't. In the end I removed the whole lot from them and my printers found another firm who did the rest of the binding at once, and with only two days left to publication date I now had all the books at last. All those copies that had been ordered in the London area I delivered myself, combining calling on buyers and delivering books, and perhaps my greatest triumph was when the firm that had said they wouldn't buy a copy actually ordered five hundred on publication. I wonder whether other authors feel as proud as I did when I saw my books in the shops? And when I was told that certain members of the royal family had bought copies, I stuck the letter in my album.

I now had a feeling that the thing to do was to get the B.B.C. to review the book for me, so with a polite note I sent them a copy. But when I asked some weeks later on the telephone whether they were going to do so, I got the reply that they only reviewed books published by well-known publishers. So I told them, sadly, that I would collect it at the reception desk if they would leave it for me. Life has strange unknown surprises in store for all of us, and it was whilst collecting this book that I got my first broadcasting chance. I was showing my book to the sympathetic receptionist at Broadcasting House when in rushed a lady in an obvious fluster. She said, 'Oh dear, I am due on in ten minutes, and I am in the midst of writing a book.' I turned to her laughingly and said: 'Give up writing a book, for I have just had mine refused for reviewing.' She looked at me and replied, 'Sit down, and I'll come and see you after my broadcast.'

I waited dutifully until she returned and looked at my book and talked to me for a few minutes. Then she said, 'You sound interesting, and I am going to get you an audition to broadcast.' She went off straight away, and when she came back she gave me the name of a producer who would see me in a few minutes and would give me an audition. I was quite flabbergasted, and before I could quite collect myself she had gone off, as she had arrived, in a tearing hurry. I was then taken up to a studio and was told to read something. I did this, but the producer came back and said that I talked far too fast, but that if I slowed down I would be excellent. He asked me to go home and write down my experiences in the Argentine. What I wrote was: 'The kind way to break horses', and a few weeks later I did my first broadcast, which was repeated a week later. Dozens of letters came in to me and to the B.B.C. afterwards, and since then I have done many other broadcasts. But I have never again met my benefactor, and I have often wondered whether she realizes what she did for that unknown dairy farmer that I was in those days.

It was now I decided that my dog should be a film star. I began by teaching her everything I could, and she was simply marvellous, for it took only a minute or two to teach her something new. But tragedy was upon me once more: she had developed cancer of the leg, and within three weeks had become a quite hopeless case. We knew that she would have to be put down eventually, and my husband suggested that I should get another puppy before this tragedy happened, so that I should have another dog to comfort me. I didn't know what to do and often cried myself to sleep over the thought of putting down such a lovely dog when she didn't appear to be suffering. But an X-ray photograph showed a rapid bone growth and the veterinary college told me there was no hope for her.

I then bought a miserable, terrified little Great Dane puppy, my only reason for buying her being her obvious unhappiness, and my maternal instinct wanting to protect her. I brought her home and she and Jyntee soon loved each other greatly, although I often thought I saw a look of sadness in Jyntee's eyes. No reader who has not had to sentence a dog to death will be able to understand what my feelings were when I knew I must send my dog to happier hunting grounds. But I will pass over my agony of spirit as I gave her the capsules that sent her to sleep with her head on my lap.

I called my new puppy Juno, and all the love for dogs I possessed now went to Juno, who from about ten weeks old became almost like a human being to me – just as if the spirit of Jyntee had passed to her. As her rickety legs grew straight, and her cries of terror, as I went to pick her up, ceased, she became a normal puppy. I don't know what her former life had been, but I knew what her future would be with us: she should become the cleverest and most intelligent dog in the world! At seven months old she did a little film for Pathé showing all the things she could do, and I still have a 16-mm. copy of it which I greatly treasure.

And it was not long after this that, at an agricultural show, I saw dogs doing obedience tests. They quite fascinated me, and I went home and taught Juno most of what I had seen. Then I decided to join two clubs where these dogs learnt this work, for, although I had trained dogs all my life, I had never yet done this specific work. Juno learnt so quickly that in three weeks she beat her instructor in a competition at a show, and a few months later she was beating dogs that had been at it for years. Now was the time, in my opinion, to build up her reputation, and once more I was determined to make my dog a film star.

If only things would go according to plan, how nice it would be! But about this time I began to get a severe pain in my chest on any exertion, and if I went upstairs I had to pause for breath. When I took my bull out to grass, if he jumped for joy it caused me a severe pain in my left arm with the effort of holding him. My husband and I knew very well what it was: years of overwork, and maybe my illness in the Argentine, had caused my old heart to protest. I got worse rapidly, until I was afraid to do almost anything. It was clear that the cows would have to be reduced in number and my bulls would have to go altogether. But what was I to do with them? One couldn't just shoot young, healthy, high-yielding cows. The bulls were an easier matter: friends wanted them, but my cows had always worn rugs, and I knew that no ordinary person would carry this on and that they would soon catch chills. Luck, however, was with me this time, and a cattle-dealing friend offered to take all the cows I wished to part with and to keep them himself, and promised to keep their rugs on them until the summer, when it would be warm enough to discard them altogether. I think he did this out of kindness, as he knew what a distressing thing it was for me to have to part with my beautiful herd. So I kept only old Queenie and Mossie, for these two wouldn't make a lot of work, and I must have something to do or I'd go mad, and complete rest for me would be sheer purgatory. I decided to slim, feeling that if I were quite thin I wouldn't have so much to carry about, although the specialist I saw said he couldn't see that I was fat. However, he gave me a diet sheet and I am going to tell my readers just how difficult it is to be honest, and to slim according to the rules.

I suppose many thousands of men and women try to regain their youthful figures by giving up eating the things they like most. Some seem to be able to eat raw vegetables and starch-free bread and to like it. But I am afraid that I love chocolate, and could quite happily live on cake. So when I first glanced over the diet that was to be mine for the next few weeks it simply appalled me. One piece of toast and an egg for breakfast, after one has milked cows and taken the dogs for a run on the common, seemed starvation to me; but I suppose that is what it was meant to be, so I decided to treat this dieting just as I would have done an experiment with my cows, and, if I found out anything particularly interesting, I would tell anyone who wanted to know.

Well I did make an interesting discovery : that the urge to eat, with me at any rate, comes only at the times when one has been accustomed to eating normally; but what is not generally known is that the urge to eat more than you are allowed lasts for only about twenty minutes. That means that if one eats one's single piece of toast, and then hastily gets up from the table and goes to do something where one can't get any food, or if some kind friend rings one up and talks for the next twenty minutes, the urge to cheat and to eat more food soon disappears. This was extremely useful to me, for my hunger was wicked. I think I have always eaten quite well, for I tend to rush about and I am sure that I burn up a lot of calories; but I should hate to count the number of bars of chocolate I have eaten in my lifetime. By eating no potatoes, bread, butter, sugar, jam, or puddings, and by confining myself to four bits of Ryvita a day for breakfast and tea, and by eating stacks of fruit, I found I could lose a pound and a half a day. But I wonder whether other slimming folk steal into the larder when they hope no one is looking, and with the guiltiest of consciences to eat just one cake? One always does this when one hopes the family won't know! But I rather enjoy the feeling of being a strong-willed martyr in this matter, and my moral courage seems to me distinctly low when I sink to sneaking food in-between meals. It took me fifteen days to lose eighteen pounds in weight, and I put the success of the thing down to never sitting for more than about two minutes at any meal. Immediately I had bolted my mouse-sized allowance, I got up and left the family and went and wrote letters, or took the dogs for a walk. I never bought any chocolate and begged the children to eat up theirs as quickly as they could, for to have to buy the children's ration and not to eat any myself was for me a severe test of self-control.

The diet did me a lot of good. I got quite thin and I felt much better, and I could once more walk upstairs without having to pause for breath half-way. One day, however, I had a horrid experience: I got a sudden and severe pain when I was picking something up off the floor. I managed to crawl to the telephone to call a doctor, but as it was in the middle of the afternoon no doctor was in although I tried three. One maid brightly suggested that I should come to the surgery at six that night. I wondered then whether, when my husband was in general practice, our maid had made such bright suggestions! It was indeed lucky for me that my husband came home shortly after that, somewhat earlier than usual, and quickly gave his already blue wife a heart stimulant, or this book would not have been written. Talking about being ice calm in emergencies, I remember once avoiding a skidding bus and missing it by inches whilst driving my car. Having escaped a collision, I was just saying how lucky we were when I went into a front-wheel skid myself, and out of control headed for a drop at the side of the road. I remember quietly telling my husband that we were going to turn over, which gave him time to put his hands on the roof, and although we did turn over we suffered nothing more than shock. Once our house was struck by lightning; once a woman died at my feet at a dog show; and on another occasion a raving lunatic arrived at our house with the fixed intention of murdering Hilda my cook, a situation that needed tactful handling to say the least of it. Police apparently cannot come to lunatics on private premises unless murder is committed, and it seemed an eternity before I got help from the asylum. But in every case I remember feeling ice cold and clear headed.

I think I inherited from my mother this ice-cold manner that comes to me in real emergencies, for I remember once, when she and I were in church together, suddenly seeing the wall over the parson's head beginning to crack. I watched for a few seconds to make sure, then shouted to the parson and to the choir to jump for their lives as the wall was coming down. It never occurred either to my mother or to me to attempt to move ourselves, but there was a terrible rush for the door which, of all awful things, opened inwards. Old people were knocked down and trampled on, and it wasn't until then that I felt such fury at what was going on that I fought like a tiger to push people away in order to get the door open. The more they lost their heads the worse the danger became, not only from the falling masonry but from the crush and the risk of being trampled on. What a terrible thing panic is. It is the same with animals when a stampede occurs: animals get killed and trampled on and die.

Little by little I got much better, and as I got better I wanted to be up and doing. So, as my farm no longer took up all my time, I decided to give road-safety demonstrations to schools and cinema audiences, and to anyone else who would like to see how dogs should be trained. This led to Juno becoming quite well known, and I started to keep a press-cuttings book for her.

13   Discoursing with Animal Film-stars

By this time, my Great Dane Juno had all four feet firmly implanted in the artistic world. This was just as well, for one day in 1951 Pinewood Studios rang up to say that they were making a picture called *Appointment with Venus*, a story of a cow, and they wanted a new-born calf to act a small part in the film. They said they wanted it on Monday morning, that it must be a bull calf, and not more than forty-eight hours old. Could I supply it? What a request! How could I know if a bull calf would be born at precisely the right time! It reminded me vividly of my own experiences with the War Agricultural Committee. However, here at last was a chance to get my nose inside a film studio legally, so I said 'Yes', and that I would have it there exactly when they wanted it. Luckily I knew a great many owners of herds, so I rang up several of them and found that most of them had near-calving cows. They all promised to telephone me as soon as a bull calf arrived. My luck was in, for on the Saturday evening a bull was born three miles away. I bought it at once and fetched it home early on the Sunday morning, for I felt that if I did this job really well they might eventually want a dog – and Juno certainly could act.

It was exciting having to get to the studios so very early in the morning, although it was extremely inconvenient for me, as I had to get up at crack of dawn to milk Mossie and Queenie, and then arrange to get the children to school by taxi. But it was all finally arranged and I bundled the calf into the car with me – and Juno came too. We were duly saluted by the gatekeeper as we sailed in, but nobody seemed to know anything and nobody seemed to care whether we stayed or not. In fact, in a very short time, I realized why it is that films cost such a lot of money! The calf was not actually wanted that day at all, so I just sat around and watched the filming, and the impression I got was that there were a great many people about, all doing exceedingly little. I talked to one lady who apparently just knits all day watching her young charge who is acting in the film.

It was many days later that my calf was finally wanted, and by that time, of course, he was too old, so I had to find another one. Once again I managed to produce a newborn bull calf, whose part it was just to lie about near its film mother and to look new-born! Not so the cow. She had to lie down when she didn't want to, and to look as if she had just had a calf. She had to be roped and thrown, and that was where I came in. Unofficially, I stayed with her, stroking her and calming her, whilst everyone got ready, and fortunately she liked my stroking and was quite content to stay still – but only while I was with her, and when I left her she felt very differently. I am afraid making films with animals is not an easy thing to do, and I knew there and then that I would never let Juno do anything she didn't really like doing. So my first visit to a film studio left me bored stiff with the wasted hours one sits around, and impressed by one thing only – that nobody was allowed to do anything at all that he wasn't actually employed to do. I remember bringing the cow for them up the studio-made cliff path, and finding scenery which consisted of a truss of hay blocking the cow's way. I asked a man to chuck it overboard, but he looked at me in horror, saying that he was an electrician and that that was a 'prop's' job. But I suggested that anyone could lift a truss of hay and would he please take it out of the cow's way. He gave me a withering look and walked away, so I picked it up and chucked it over the edge, narrowly missing a star or two down below. As far as I could see, if the cow had been hanging herself, they'd have had to wait for the props department to get a knife to cut her down.

I was a fortnight on that job, but in the finished picture my calf appeared for a matter only of seconds. No wonder films cost such vast sums to produce!

A little later I really thought Juno's chance had come. Metro-Goldwyn-Mayer Studios rang up for her to go to Cornwall to act in the film *Never Let Me Go*, starring Clark Gable and Gene Tierney. I went over to the studios at Elstree to show them the dog and they said it was just the animal they needed. I was in the middle of haymaking at the time, and I was worried about what would happen to the hay if they called me before it was finished. And that is just what did actually happen: Would I be in Cornwall by the very next evening? So I sold my hay for a song to a neighbour, no sacrifice being too great if Juno was going to be a film star. An hour before I was due to leave, they rang up again and said the schedule had changed and would I wait until they notified me when to go. I had to wait a whole fortnight, and bitterly regretted having sold my hay, but at last the summons came. My husband got off from the hospital for the ten days we were to be away and off we went. My second sight worried me all the time, telling me that it would never come off. But this time I just refused to listen, for surely now that I was off with the dog nothing *could* go wrong? We arrived at eleven o'clock at night, and were shown to our digs.

A week or two earlier my little daughter Judith had bought a little black-and-tan terrier bitch to train herself, only eight weeks old, and we had felt that we had better bring her to Cornwall with us as well for fear that her training might suffer if she were left at home. When we arrived, we were told that we should eat at the hotel, but would have to sleep in digs. I don't know how they got the word sleep mixed up with the digs we were given, for the first night we put our tired heads on the pillows we

thought somebody must have got some studio cement
mixed up in the mattress. It felt just like sand; if one
pushed terribly hard, one could just dent it slightly. I had
the idea of putting Juno to lie on it, hoping that with her
great weight she might be able to make a hole. But no, she
wouldn't stay there for a second and much preferred the
floor. We fought all night for the single blanket, and the
cast-iron pillows were soon on the floor. Why, oh why had
I become film-struck! We thought lovingly of our comfortable bedroom at home, and tossed and turned all night to
the accompaniment of snores from the occupants of the
room next door. At five o'clock I got up and took the dogs
out, my husband in the meantime having dropped off into
a restless doze. I quite wished that I hadn't slimmed, for if
I had been better padded I might just have been able to
stand up to this assault course!

The dawn was incredibly beautiful. There was a full moon
and the June air was soft and scented. I walked for miles.
The dogs thought it funny but they were quite willing to
come with me. When I got back, about an hour later, I
found everything in a great bustle. Apparently everyone
has to be on the set on location at 7.45. We went over to
the hotel for breakfast, and met some of the camera men
and other important back-room boys, but we found that we
were not on call that day – according to the schedule.

Later that day we went down to the cove at Mullion to
watch the filming, and everyone greatly admired Juno. It
was very lovely down there, but we were on edge, for we
had thought they were going to use us straight away, and
waiting about has always killed me. That night the orders
for the following morning were posted up, and Juno and
Mrs Woodhouse were down to be at Gunwalloe Cove next
morning at 7.45. The fact that the night held little sleep
for me on that grave-like bed didn't seem to matter now.
We breakfasted bright and early and went in the car the
few miles to the appointed spot. There wasn't a soul there
when we arrived, and we found the virgin sand washed

spotless, except for horrid little patches of tar which stuck to everything. We sat down to wait, and presently two big vans rolled down, and a few hikers also, who had heard that filming was to be done there and wanted to see for themselves in reality this strange thing called film-making.

Men started laying great cables from the top of the cliff, bringing power for the great arc lamps needed for the filming, and the two caravans carrying the stars turned up next and were parked in a field nearby. That was where the stars would stay until they were wanted for the actual filming, for stand-ins do all the tiring standing about and the taking-up of camera positions before the actual shooting. More people kept arriving and soon the rocks and cliffs were getting perilously crowded with film fans who craned their necks over the edge of the cliff, sending little stones hurtling down onto those below. A small boy rushed up to Clark Gable's stand-in, thinking it was the great star himself, and asked for his autograph, while more and more people continued to arrive: make-up people, director, producer, dancing director, etc., and property men in vast numbers, who had the awful job of trying to make the sand look as if the tide had just washed it. They had buckets of water and brushes to do this with, but people would not stop walking over their handiwork. Patiently they again and again washed and brushed out the footsteps. Cameras were now being set up and the tension grew. Babies began to cry here and there and got slapped by their film-struck mothers. Slightly bigger children begged in whining voices for Daddy to go and build sand-castles; but Daddy wanted to see if Gene Tierney was all he hoped she would be, and nothing was going to budge him until his curiosity was satisfied. The arc lights suddenly flashed into being, and soon the great generators were doing their bit on this fantastic stage that had been set up in such beautiful natural surroundings.

People kept coming and talking to Juno, who really wanted to sleep. Was she in the film? Could they photograph her? And press-men asked me questions about what she ate. Soon there was quite a crowd round her; but suddenly we all sprang to attention, for the stars were approaching, and necks craned more dangerously than ever over the cliffside. A rope was run up to protect the actors from losing what little clothing they wore, this being a bathing-costume scene. Great reflectors were now being hauled up the cliff to reflect the sun and to make the film sharp. The words 'Quiet, please', from the producer, made us all quiver with excitement. I asked what Juno was supposed to do, but nobody seemed to know or care, so I just sat down again. My experiences at Pinewood had taught me just to wait and say nothing, for film executives move in a mysterious way.

The crowd was getting restless; they wanted action, and so far the only action they had seen was the constant washing away by props of any footmarks on the sand. But all was now set, and eyes were anxiously scanning the sky. The sun, which shortly before had been shining so brightly, now hid shyly behind clouds. Once more it came out, and once more the producer shouted. 'Get ready for shooting, all quiet please.' The actors took up their position for a love scene; last-minute tapes measured the distances from the cameras; the photometers gave the exposure necessary, and then finally the director bellowed 'Action'. A second later he called 'Cut', for the sun had gone, and everyone gasped with annoyance. Hundreds of eyes scanned the now rather overcast sky, to find on the horizon a small patch of blue which seemed kindly to be heading our way. Meanwhile, restless people walked again over the washed sand, watched by the men of the props department with unbelievable patience and without a word of reproach, who then again brushed all the marks out.

A bell went. Morning tea break! Surely they weren't going to drink tea with that blue sky approaching? This I asked someone obviously connected with the film, and he assured me, with a pained expression, that of course they were going to break for tea – union rules.

I took the dogs down to the sea. A sharp wind had got up and I shivered a little. Little patches of blue came and went and nobody cared. There was then no more blue sky to be seen anywhere, so everyone sat down again, and odd people – the director among them – came and talked pleasantly to us and admired the dog. Several admirers asked what she had got to do, and I felt rather silly when I said that I didn't know. The crowd brought out their sandwiches; babies grew exhausted and fell asleep; cyclists hauled their bicycles up the dangerous rocks; and props kept on and on washing the sand. Then the lunch bell went, and we all ate a wonderful lunch, ending up with strawberries. By now I felt near to a nervous breakdown – surely we must *soon* be going to do *something*? But no, the tide was already turning and it was nearly four o'clock.

Then, all of a sudden, someone pointed to a large patch of blue that was appearing on the horizon, and everyone again got excited. The stars were called from their caravans; the crowd milled about once more; and more stones came hurtling down. Some of the spectators hadn't minded what they were doing and now had great lumps of tar sticking to themselves. The cameras were lined up again; focuses were taken; and the producer called for silence as the sun came out. 'Action' called the director once more, only to follow with 'Cut', for something wasn't quite right yet. The tea bell was the next event, and in a second everyone had left what he was doing, and buns and tea completely occupied all their minds. Once more brilliant sun held the clouds at bay, what we had waited for all day long, and surely they were going to shoot *now*? But once again, no, apparently not, for tea must always come first.

When that was over, further shooting for that day was clearly impossible, since the tide had now compelled a decision. The disappointed crowd could hardly believe their eyes as the props men stopped washing and brushing the sand, the stars retired to their caravans, and the great lights were taken down. The sun was brilliant now, but nobody seemed to want it. The fretful babies got slapped harder than ever to make up for their mothers' disappointment; Father hadn't made up his mind whether his favourite film star could really act; and little Tommy had long since wandered off and had made rows of castles by himself. Lastly the great generators wound their weary way back the five miles they had come from their parking places. The tide now lapped the rocks, and we set off once more for the hotel, there being nothing else now to do.

The schedule for the following day was duly posted up in the hotel. This time Juno and I were not included, and the waiting became even more irksome. I gathered that they wanted a shimmer on the sea for the taking of the scenes with Juno, and this could only be procured with a cloudless sky.

The next day dawned clear and bright, without a cloud to be seen, and surely just the very day for our scene? I made enquiries, but gathered that they never altered a schedule. Today was the day for blowing up a boat's cabin, and it would be blown up whatever happened.

The day after that Juno and I were again on call. The weather looked doubtful to me, but we sailed off to the same beach again.

This time we did get two simple scenes done, and my spirits rose. But now I wished the actors knew their parts better! Juno never forgot what *she* had to do herself, and when one actor said that the dog made him forget his lines I felt simply furious. After these two scenes, the weather became hopeless, and we were all told that there would be no more shooting that day. So we spent the rest of the day in nearby towns selling my books to booksellers. But this idleness over the film was really killing. Day after day the weather refused to come right, and the company had stayed there longer than they had reckoned, which meant that the hotels and digs began to tell us that they had new visitors booked to come and that we couldn't stay any longer.

For the ten days we remained there, nothing more was done; and in the end we were all told to go home, and that the film would now be made in the studios. Was my second sight going to be right in the end after all, I wondered? And that, to our great disappointment, was how it actually turned out, for a fortnight later I heard that they had scrapped Juno's part altogether and done a scene of a lake instead, and as they felt that a big dog couldn't act safely on a raft they had had very regretfully to cut her out. I was more than heartbroken, for everyone who knew us knew that Juno was to be acting in the film, and I felt they would think that she had failed in her part. But in films nobody cares about what hurt comes to people's feelings – and that was that.

Not long after this episode the Shepperton Studios rang up for a dog to appear in *Sea Devils*. I took Juno down to see them and they told me they had been trying for ages to get a 'boxer' to do the little piece that was wanted, but he just wouldn't. Juno, however, did it first shot and made me feel very pleased. She for her part enjoyed the fuss made of her, and I the twelve pounds that we got for that one day's work! When I saw the film I wondered why they had wanted a dog at all – they'd cut the incident so much. But that was not my business.

This new nibble at the film industry made me keener than ever to make Juno a star. I longed for her to be the Lassie of the English screen, and people certainly love animal films.

I was walking one day down Piccadilly when I saw a plate up which said 'British Films Ltd.', and, as I had an hour or so to spare, I went in. I asked to see the manager and refused to state my business for the simple reason that I hadn't really any idea yet of what I was going to suggest. However, the secretary clearly liked Juno and we were allowed to go in. What I suggested, on the spur of the moment, was that it was high time that some film company made attractive films in the Lassie style, and I proposed Juno as the star. The manager said that he quite agreed with me but that films were expensive things to make, and that unless one could get a sponsor one could do nothing.

However, he suggested that I should go round to their production side and have a talk with them there. I did this, and told them all that Juno could do, left my name and address, and hoped above hope that something would come of it – and something did. The director wrote a script, suitable for a children's film, called *Juno Helps Out*, and sent it in to the Children's Film Foundation. He wrote the script after paying us a visit one day and discussing with me the sort of things that Juno could do. Our luck was in, for the Foundation had enough money left to do one short twenty-minute film and the script was accepted. The company decided it would be best if the film were shot at my home, and agreed to my two children, Judith and Patrick, taking the leading parts in it with Juno.

All was fixed up in a businesslike manner, and the film unit duly turned up 'on location' at Campions, where we now lived. Never have I seen such a lot of stuff! First of all it was all brought down for one day only to do a film test with the children. A huge camera filled our kitchen, and the cook was given the day off. Dozens of lamps of all sizes filled the house, the small ones being nicknamed 'pups', which amused Patrick. Finally, a large recording van from Associated British Pathé filled our yard, and cables were run everywhere. The kitchen scene was short, showing the two children of the house carrying on, with the help of Juno, all the household tasks while their mother was ill. In this scene Patrick was the dunderhead who always meant well, while Judith, his elder sister, was scolding him for what he did wrong, and Juno helped out at the right moments. In one part, as the children are washing up, Patrick lets a plate fall and break on the floor, and, after doing it, raising his eyes in a pathetic way and throwing his hands up like a Frenchman, says in apprehensive tone, 'It slipped'. The way he did it made us all laugh, but at seven years old I think most children are born film-stars. This first test came through with flying colours, and a few weeks afterwards the filming began in earnest. I gathered that they would be with us daily from about nine until six for a whole month. There seemed to be an awful lot of people about: director, producer, continuity girl, electrician, camera man, sound technicians, etc., and soon there was a complete upheaval of normal life at Campions.

I often felt that my training in the Argentine, when I used sometimes to have to prepare meals at a moment's notice, served me well. Shooting seldom stopped in the kitchen before one o'clock, when I had to dash in hastily to prepare a meal for the five of us, and then be ready for shooting again at two o'clock. In the meantime the unit went to a restaurant in the town for their own meal.

I had been given a copy of the script and used to teach Juno the day before what she was wanted to do – things like pulling the children's bedclothes off, and going shopping by herself. One of the funniest things that I taught her was to pick up her shopping basket, whilst sitting in a queue alone in a shop, and every time the queue moved up to pick her basket up and move up with the others. She had to bark when the milk boiled over; take a dinner tray up to the sick mother who was in bed; submit to being bathed in soapflakes, and then, all wet, to jump on Mother's bed, and many other amusing incidents – and she simply loved it. Directly the director said 'Action', she knew at once exactly what was wanted, and I never once saw her make a mistake. When he said 'Cut', she rushed all over the place, barking excitedly, as much as to say 'I did it well, didn't I?'

Once the director forgot to say what a clever girl she was and she was hopelessly upset. One has to remember with animals that they work for praise, and one must never forget to tell them how clever they are all the time. It is fatal also to repeat an action too many times, or the dog will get bored stiff. Juno was always best when the first take was all right; but of course this was not always possible, for the children were also amateurs, and it was often that technical things caused a retake.

Our domestic life in the meantime was simply dreadful : great cables ran through windows, and we had to sleep with them half open, our bed at night often being surrounded with lights and a huge camera. But it was wonderful actually to be making a film at last with Juno in it, and the children were getting on well, and the 'rushes' (or quick looks), of the daily sequences we were taking, were very encouraging. We did all the sound parts first, because the sound is the expensive part of the film and they wanted to let the sound men go. The outdoor shots were then taken with a smaller camera and this could be done at any time when the weather was right.

At last the actual filming was completed, and we could hardly wait to see the film finished; but it takes a long time apparently to cut and edit a film and we had to be very patient. But the great day arrived in the end and we went up to London for the private viewing. It was all we hoped for and expected, and the general reaction of the public who saw it was, 'Oh, what a pity it has ended, it's too short.' The preview was put on at a big cinema and the children and Juno went onto the stage to meet their public. There Juno did a trick or two, like picking her own name out of the alphabet, just to show how clever she was. She is always ready to pose for photographers, but goes quite mad after the flash is over and tears round everyone in a most boisterous way showing off.

I find it quite impossible to understand people who say that dogs don't like doing tricks. Juno simply adores being clever, and she has the most lovely expression of pride when she has done something really well. All dogs, in my opinion, should have work of some kind to do, such as working sheep or police work, or whatever else one can find for them. And that is why I think obedience training is so good for them, as it gives them an object to work for.

14 The Dogs and I train the Dog-trainers

After this film was finished I went back to my road safety work, and at other times went collecting with Juno carrying her boxes for the Sunshine Homes for Blind Babies. I used to go miles and miles giving demonstrations to schools and women's guilds, and so on, and then one day I did a twelve-minute programme with Juno on television, showing how a dog should be trained. I had dozens of letters from viewers after that, all wanting to know how to train their dogs, and that gave me the idea that perhaps locally I should start a class to show people how to train their dogs.

I began by going to see the local Road Safety Officer to ask him about letting me give a demonstration, and about getting a hall so that we could show a film or two about dogs. I also wished to invite people to bring their bad dogs along, and I would guarantee to make them behave properly within two minutes by the clock. I invited the press to see how it was done, and the following note appeared beforehand in the *Watford Observer*. 'There is an open invitation for members of the public to take untrained dogs on the platform, when Mrs Woodhouse will demonstrate what can be done in two minutes. Judging from past experience I have had with dogs – mongrel and thoroughbred – I for one will be surprised if any training at all can be done in that time. However, I am willing to be convinced, and I must add that when Mrs Woodhouse spoke to me on the subject she sounded extremely confident.' When the time came, the hall was packed and many people found they couldn't get in. The Road Safety Officer was much surprised, as he had assured me that you would never get more than fifty people at a time to go to any meeting. I began by giving a demonstration with Juno, then with other people's dogs, sixteen in all coming up for me to tackle, and without exception I did as I had promised, getting all those dogs to behave properly in the timed two minutes. I then handed them back to their owners, and they again behaved very badly. That was what I had expected, and it went to show that it was the owners who were at fault and not the dogs; it was just that the owners lacked the knowledge of how to handle their dogs properly.

After this preliminary success, I straightaway launched a training club at Croxley Green, managing to get the Territorial parade ground to train on, the classes to be on Sunday afternoons. Seven members came to the first class, and we showed them how to start. But the numbers rose each week and eventually there were forty dogs altogether that used to come from time to time. By now we were getting quite well known: we would give demonstrations with the members' dogs, and television newsreel once took a film of our class. This led to my starting another branch in Cassiobury Park in Watford, and then another at Ickenham.

The work fascinated me. Here were dozens of dogs and dog-owners, no doubt loving each other, but in almost every case they were opposing each other in their ideas of how their lives should be lived. Some dogs pulled unmercifully on the lead, one big Airedale arriving with its mistress in front carrying a stick and its master hanging on like grim death, with his hand nearly eaten to the bone by the lead that was attached to the dog. When we put a choke chain collar on this dog, he tried his best to be sick to pay us out. He certainly was a tremendous weight to handle, and the necessary jerks that had to be given to stop him pulling on the lead nearly dislocated my back. But little by little he became a more normal dog, and soon learnt to sit and wait whilst his owner went out of sight. He also learnt to pay no attention to other dogs, and hardest of all to teach him, he learnt to retrieve a dumb-bell. I don't think I have ever had such a stubborn dog either before or since. He knew perfectly well what was wanted of him, but had no intention at all of doing it unless the spirit moved him, and we used to take him along to all our demonstrations with us as the clown. We'd give a guardsman-like demonstration with about a dozen dogs, Juno being among them, and Jumbo would do everything right but only in his own time. He would sniff along half-way towards his master, when being called; the crowd would laugh, and then one could almost swear that Jumbo smiled, as he gave a cunning look at his master: 'Smack me if you dare,' he almost leered, for the crowd doesn't like to see any dog smacked, however much he deserves it. At the end of the show, the guardsman-like handlers and the dogs got a good round of applause; and, as Jumbo was almost frog-marched off by his irritated owner, he too got thunderous applause, which all goes to show that the average person really enjoys watching a disobedient dog. And it is quite extraordinary how dogs *do* play up in crowds.

I often used to go with Juno to obedience tests at shows, not because I like them for I don't – in fact I loathe them – but if I was to become a successful dog club trainer I must first of all prove to the public that my own dog is capable of competing in and winning the stiffest tests. But how often has my dog become dull and listless when taking part in these tests, while at home she is the fastest thing on four legs. She seems to me to sense my being nervous, and that makes her nervous too.

In these competitions, one is only allowed a single command by word or signal. What a miserable rule! For surely the real test of dog and owner should be one of brains and ingenuity. But now see what happens when a supposed burglar offers the dog a piece of meat, which she isn't supposed to take from a stranger: at first she refuses, then it may happen, as it did to Juno the other day, that the pseudo-burglar tried to stroke her – she snapped at him, and lost two marks. Why, oh why? Is a dog not to take meat from a burglar yet to allow him to caress her? What is to stop him slipping a rope over her head and tying her up, if she allows such liberties? Juno was the only dog among the whole lot really to use her head. As long as the man kept his distance, she paid no attention, but no fondling for this lady, for she knows her job.

If I dare to smile encouragement to her whilst she is working, off come more marks, for that counts as an extra signal. Or if I sway my body slightly, in giving her an order from a long distance, with the effort not only of shouting the command but of willing her to carry it out, off come more marks again. I certainly love working dogs, but why not let us do it with all the fun in our voices and our eyes that we normally use to train them? To the dungeons, I say, with all these statuesque handlers, whose dogs pleadingly watch their masters' faces for the faintest sign of approval while they are working, and nothing is going to stop me smiling at my dogs in these tests, when I think they have done well. I shall will them to do the right thing, and, if a word of praise from me loses me a mark, I would rather lose a hundred marks than the love of my dog.

What an exciting experience it is, running a dog club! Every dog and every owner has his separate problem. Certainly no two dogs are alike, and I remember one dear little very nervous black-and-tan miniature who learnt very quickly all the ordinary exercises, but she would not leave her mistress to go and fetch the dumb-bell – she would go just a pace or two and then rush back to safety. Her mistress was getting very worried about it, because she thought her little dog would never get over it. I decided to kneel on the floor and, as she was sent to fetch the dumb-bell, I would tell her what a wonderful little person she was and encourage her to come to me and pick it up. I used my tenderest, tiniest voice to tell her all was well, and when she came to me I kissed her and told her to pick it up. She did so, and then rushed back to her mistress with her tail wagging fifty to the dozen. After that I only had to stand near the dumb-bell, and encourage her in that same voice, for her to come and pick it up at once. Soon I let her do it by herself; if she hesitated, even though she couldn't see me, I only had to say 'Judy, pick it up' to give her back her confidence. If only owners really would sometimes get on their knees, and love their dogs when they are nervous, what a difference it would make.

It was whilst running these dog clubs that I realized how hopelessly small my efforts were in this land of disobedient dogs. This was brought home to me by the hundreds of letters from desperate owners of disobedient dogs that I got after the broadcasts on my work that I gave at this time. Dogs that won't come when called; dogs that chew things up; dogs that bark incessantly; dogs that bite their owners – and perhaps it was this last category that staggered me most, for there were literally dozens of owners who wrote to me sadly saying that they are contemplating putting their dogs down owing to this spiteful biting trick. They seemed to think that biting the postman was fair game, but that, when it came to biting their babies or themselves, it was quite a different matter.

Then there is the dog-owner who never sees his dog from early morning until late at night. I have many of those dogs on my place, when my bitches are indisposed, and I get furious telephone calls from owners who ask me why I don't send my bitch to kennels when she is in that state, and who get wild when I suggest that the answer is for them to control their own dogs and to leave me and mine in peace.

Many dog-owners ask me why I haven't rung them up when their dogs have come round to my home – but would they, I wonder, pay for my telephone calls! Their dogs come and dig up my garden, chase my cat, kill my chickens, and make my front door smell – but I am to have no compensation. One actually broke one of my glasshouse windows the other day, and when I asked its owner for the five shillings to repair it, he became abusive about my dogs attracting his. I assured him that there was no reason for his dog to come round here at all. Why is it that some dog-owners must do their best to make one hate dogs altogether?

But I became sorry for these ignorant dog-owners, and set out to raise the money to make a film on my work in the field of dog training. First of all I tried the usual lazy method of asking the animal societies for help and big firms for subscriptions, but I drew a blank. Then I decided to run an enormous 'August Fair', as I called it, on my farm, with 'stupendous attractions', so I gathered together a committee of dog lovers to help me. I chose a date when I felt it would be reasonably fine and then set about organizing it. I felt that a pony gymkhana, a motor-cycle gymkhana with jumping and obstacle races and other exciting features, would amuse a certain section of a crowd, and to keep the others entertained I arranged for a big fun fair, a tombola, a children's pet show, a dog obedience match, and lastly but not least a top-class mannequin parade.

Readers may think this quite an easy thing to do, but believe me the work entailed was colossal. I had to collect, by begging, over six hundred articles for the tombola, and in addition to that to arrange all the catering, hire all the ropes which were needed to comply with the rules of the official motor-cycling associations, get jumps and other things for the ponies, chairs for the crowd which would we hoped watch the dogs working, tents for first aid, platforms and dressing rooms for the mannequins, and lastly a gigantic loud-speaker system to cover the ten acres of my farm. I begged or cajoled everyone I met into doing something to help, and before I had finished I had sold a thousand tickets for the show, going from door to door selling a single ticket for a shilling or a book of six for three shillings and six-pence – by doing this I hoped to cover the whole of the outgoing expenses.

To cut a long story short, everything went off more or less according to plan, and we were able to start off my

Canine Road Safety Film Fund with a sum of one hundred and twenty-four pounds. It had cost one hundred and eighty-six pounds to put the fair on, otherwise our profit would have been a bigger one. But, thank heaven, the weather was fine – a wet day would have seen me taking a job as a char for many years to come in order to pay off the debts, for I was the sole backer. I continued to collect for my fund whenever possible, on one occasion taking Juno to a football match with a box on her back and collecting six pounds in the interval, and on another by running a comic dog show on the beach at Polzeath, whilst on holiday, followed by races for old and young also on the beach. I ran bazaars, and also made hundreds of Christmas cards and sold them to club members. I did demonstrations with my dogs at Acton carnival, and anywhere else where people would collect together. Bit by bit the fund rose; and in the end I found a film company who undertook to do the film at cost price, and we finally set out to do it.

I didn't want a short film, but a really comprehensive one that would show owners from beginning to end how to train their dogs. We collected about sixty of our members to appear in the film, and eventually we got down to the shooting. This time I was myself doing the film-making, and it wasn't long before I began to realize all the snags in the job. Luckily the weather remained perfect and we were able to get all the shots done within a month, working only at week-ends.

Then I heard no more about the film for some time, as the company had to go on to another assignment, and we had to wait our turn patiently, since they were doing everything at cost price. However, at last it was ready. I entitled it *Love Me, Love My Dog*, and held its preview in Watford. The audience liked it, and this, my first effort at film-making, is now likely to be seen all over the country. I also made a gramophone record of the exercises a dog should do, so I feel that anyone genuinely anxious for guidance in the business of training his dog can no longer plead that such advice does not exist.

While all this was in progress, my dog clubs were growing and growing. We now had over five hundred dogs on the books, and I opened another branch at Harrow, in the park. I had great difficulty at first in getting the officials to allow me to do anything, but in the end I discovered that there was no law or by-law to stop one doing dog training in the park, provided that one didn't cause a nuisance. So I informed the powers-that-be that I was making a start, and I think they soon realized that we were not going to dig up the flower beds or cause a riot, and in the end they gave us their blessing. They even offered to help us pay for a hall in the winter for twelve classes.

15   Snow Queen:
Film-star among Cows

Another film company rang me up soon after this to ask
if I had a cow that would allow a racing car nearly to run
into it without causing it to move. It appears that they had
been trying for weeks, in Austria, to get this small scene
done, but without success, and they had just heard that I
had some very well-behaved cows. I questioned them to
make sure that there was no risk to the cow and they were
able to reassure me about that. I well knew that my Snow
Queen, old Queenie's daughter, would do anything I told
her, so I agreed to let them come down as proposed.

When they came, I walked Snow Queen along the road
with me, until we came to a lonelier part which might be
thought to look like Austria, and the film director then
asked me to get the cow to stand still in the middle of the
road with its head-collar off, and to persuade her not to
move when the car approached at high speed with the
camera on top. I said I thought she would do that if he
gave me time to teach her what to do. The first time we did
it, she began to follow me when I took her head-collar off;
but I put her back gently and told her to stay there. Next
time she never moved an inch, except when the car finally
stopped, when she licked its headlamps! It was quite funny
to see the film men's surprise at her behaviour. They were
kind enough to say what a pleasure it had been to work
with someone who was able to make animals do what was
wanted. They then shot another different scene and after
that they left, another part of the film *Heights of Danger*
having been finished.

Curiously enough, a few minutes after they had left, the

Douglas Fairbanks Studios rang up and wanted to know if I had a cow that could take a leading part in the film *The Charm*, which was then just about to be made at Boreham Wood. I agreed that Snow Queen would do all that they wanted, and they came over to see her. The film had an amusing story of a farm lad who fell in love with the boss's daughter, but she of course wouldn't look at him. So the lad consulted a gipsy and asked for a charm to make his lady-love fall in love with him. The charm was that he must pull a hair from his loved-one's head, put it in a jar, and take it to the third willow tree, and then at midnight wish that the lady would fall in love with him. He knew he couldn't pluck a hair from the girl's head, so he bribed her young brother to do it, with the promise that he would teach him how to snare rabbits, if he would get him a hair from his sister's head. The boy got tired of trying to snatch a hair from his sister, so seeing a Guernsey cow with roughly the same coloured tail as his sister's hair, and thinking that the farm lad would never know the difference, he plucked the hair from the cow's tail and told the lad a lie. Of course the charm worked, but it was the cow who fell in love with the lad, and not the girl, whose love he sought. It is an extremely funny film, with such incidents as when the cow turned up and watched the farm lad with her love-filled eyes. She even follows him down the road and into a pub! But eventually the young brother confesses, and the gipsy has to be consulted again, so as to lift the love charm.

I thoroughly enjoyed helping with this film, for everyone was so considerate to the cow, her every wish becoming law. She was absolutely at home on the set, and used to lie down to rest between 'pups' and cables and cameras, as if she had been doing it all her life. All the people on the production seemed to me so sensible. They would ask me the best way to get the cow to do a certain thing, and in every case she did exactly what was wanted. I hate directors who try to get animals to do unnatural things, but this picture will I am sure be a very happy one. I think my cow fell genuinely in love with Douglas Fairbanks Jr., and he was amazed at the way she behaved. But it was his gentle behaviour with her, I think, that had a lot to do with it.

Once more I settled down to my routine work, until one morning I got a cutting from a German newspaper showing a very favourite picture of mine of my two children saying their prayers, and with Juno saying hers with them too. I had to get the letter translated, but the gist of it was that the writer was a breeder of Great Danes in Germany and so much admired the lovely picture of Juno and the children, that he felt he would like to show his appreciation of it by offering me as a present a Great Dane puppy from one of his own bitches. I was very touched, but I had to refuse for two reasons: firstly, because I knew that Juno would be jealous and unhappy with another dog in the house, and secondly because it seemed to me cruel to have to put the dog in quarantine for such a long time. But he kept writing to me and showed such interest in my dogs that eventually I invited him over, in four months' time, to see our Coronation show for Great Danes, an invitation which he gladly accepted.

That meant that, as he didn't speak a word of English, I should have to learn some German, so I armed myself with *Teach Yourself German*, and for the next two or three weeks I was unapproachable – I think I even dreamt in German. I then found a German teacher, who was over here on an exchange basis, to come and talk to me. I already knew quite a lot, but I had never heard the language spoken properly, even though I had had two German prisoners with me during the war. But they, oddly enough, had always spoken excellent English! I soon found I could understand and talk quite easily with my teacher, and the time came when I had to go to meet Herr Schlegel, our guest. The dogs liked him at first sight, and it wasn't long before he took over the job of wrapping up little Chica, our miniature black-and-tan terrier, in her blanket and putting her to bed at night, as I used to do myself. When

I saw him kiss her good night, as I did, it made me wonder
whether, if all animal-lovers got together, world peace
might not be nearer than it is. Here was a man who had
been badly wounded fighting the Allies, who yet came
happily to stay in our house, and kissed our dogs good
night! He stayed for a week, and during that time we saw
for the first time all the sights of London, and Windsor
Castle. He thoroughly enjoyed the Great Dane show, and
by the time he went back, I was completely exhausted
from trying endlessly to think of conversation in German.
One night I gave a dinner party for him, all the guests
being Germans and the conversation all the time in that
language. It quite surprised me, in how short a time one can
teach oneself enough of a language to get on comfortably,
and even to enjoy it. But I expect without constant practice I shall soon forget it.

Charming references to his visit appeared in some German papers that he sent me, and I hope I succeeded in
doing just a little towards the object of us all, a better
understanding between nations.

After his visit I decided that my eldest daughter, who
had been learning German for two years at school and
couldn't yet speak it even as well as I could, had better go
to school in Switzerland to learn French and German, in
case I again had wild ideas of entertaining unknown
guests! But the trouble was, what should I do with her
pony? However, I met the headmistress, and in no time at
all we had fixed up that the pony should go off to the
school as well. I wonder if any of my readers has ever
tried to send a pony to Switzerland? If not, I don't advise
them to try, for had I been trying to smuggle contraband I
couldn't have run up against worse snags. However, the
pony eventually arrived there, some days after my daughter,
and I have now had happy letters from her saying what
fun it is to ride Freddy in the snow.

16   Talking
to your own Animals

I have hundreds of letters from animal-lovers all over the
world asking me to tell them more about this business of
'talking to animals'. They want to know whether, if shown
how to do it, others, apart from myself, can communicate with their pets so that they truly understand. They
want to know whether the breathing down my nose that
I practise with horses works with dogs. Someone even
wanted to know whether I agreed with his theory that we
all get the animals we deserve.

I don't believe that on being shown how to do it everyone can actually communicate with animals in the same
way as I do myself. There is much more to it than that:
first and foremost I think one has to have a very deep love
for all the animals one comes in contact with, and coupled
with that one must be without fear. There is nothing so
catching as fear, as I showed by my story of the church
that collapsed. Animals can pick up fear at quite a distance
away, and their hearing is far more acute than a human
being's. Think how rabbits all go to their burrows at a
thump from the buck's foot as a warning of danger, and
how the stamp of a horse's foot, and a snort, will raise
every head in the wild horse herd and cause the foals to
gallop about in fear. But things even less perceptible to us
than small sounds can make animals frightened. They seem
to me to pick up fear as a fear-thought enters the mind of
the person dealing with them. That is why horses refuse
jumps. The question as to whether they will do it or not
has entered the rider's mind and been flashed to the
horse's brain. With someone who has complete confidence

that the horse can and will get over the obstacle, this does not occur, unless the animal has grown cunning or is sick of jumping. In this book I am not of course talking of wicked or cunning animals – like wicked people, they need different treatment.

I am absolutely certain that people send out waves of love or confidence, fear or hate, according to their circumstances, and that animals are accustomed to this kind of communication between themselves, and it is quite hopeless to try to fool an animal. I have often seen people trying apparently to make their dogs do something, while in their innermost hearts they thought it unnecessary, or too hard, or even perhaps silly. They tell me the dog won't do it, but I tell them I know the dog will do what they ask provided that they are certain of it in their minds. I then take their dog myself and get it to do the exercise at once. I am quite sure that the animal picks up my trust and confidence in his good behaviour and immediately wants to please.

Haven't you often noticed that a word of praise goes much further than a scolding also with human beings, and that if you have a preconceived idea that a person is nice, nine times out of ten that person will be? That is how I feel about the bad dogs that are brought to me. I blame the owners' temperaments or methods of handling, for I believe that the dog is fundamentally a well-meaning fellow. A rather good example of this recently was a large bull mastiff brought to me as absolutely impossible to brush; he bit his owner if she attempted to do it. So I took the dog on a loose lead and said to him, 'Who's going to have a simply *lovely* brushing?' in a most excited tone of voice. He looked at me expectantly, wagging his tail hard, and I went on for a few moments, telling him he really was the luckiest dog, and so forth; and then I brushed him, and he stood quite still except for the gentle tail-wagging which he kept up. When I stopped, he turned round to look at me, and I asked him if he wanted some more. The tail wagged faster, and I brushed him again, keeping up my talking to him about how lovely he was, and how lucky. The owner had suspected he might bite her, and her fear had transmitted itself to her dog until he thought brushing must be something to fear. I on the other hand, knew the dog would *not* bite me, and transmitted confidence by voice, by telepathy, and by firm use of the brush.

Most dogs can be trained if spoken to gently and quietly, but with many, much difference in intonation must be used before they will listen and obey. I think I know how to use all the different intonations needed to attract a dog's attention, and to make him obey a command, and he seems to love my 'little voice' that I use to caress him at the end. It is an intriguing sight – and a rather embarrassing one – when my class of dogs and owners have finished an exercise, to find the dogs deserting their owners and coming to me for praise. I think the explanation of this lies in my own pleasure in their performance. The same thing happens when, in an exercise, we are trying to make a dog walk nicely to heel, for nine times out of ten he will wander away from his owner. Perhaps this is because the owner tends to let his voice sound dull. So I tell them to use a more exciting tone, as if there were rats to be found everywhere – but I seldom get the voice I want, alas!

With horses and cattle it is the same. When I breathe down my nose to say how do you do to a horse, it can hear that breath at anything up to twenty yards, for horses have the most acute sense of hearing. I always teach my horses in a whisper all the commands that are necessary, and after I have breathed my first welcome to them I find they have no fear. Then the love I have for them is transmitted through my fingers. My touch soothes them and often I have seen them shut their eyes in contentment.

Horses know in exactly the same way whether you have confidence in them, and a nervous rider can ruin a top-class jumper for many a day. Often a horse starts shying because the rider sees something rather terrifying ahead and instinctively tightens the hold on the reins or the knee grip, or even just transmits fear by telepathy; with a confident rider the horse probably would not have shied, or only have shied very little. That is why I say my method of breathing up a horse's nose would not work for everyone as a foolproof method for breaking in horses. Many people don't believe in it anyway, and therefore their chances of success are practically nil. Others would like to believe it, but can't be sure; their chances are also doubtful, for the horse will sense the doubt in their minds. Others go about it too quickly, in the firm belief that there is nothing in breaking in a horse anyway; they are what I term the 'commando' type, and horses don't like that sort of approach. I believe that this breathing removes fear, but you must not give the horse any reason to become afraid again; so it is still necessary to move firmly but gently, to speak softly, and to have abundant patience in just showing your very willing friend what he must do.

Do we get the animals we deserve? Perhaps we do, but it is a bit hard that we must suffer for our shortcomings by having nasty or stupid animals to deal with, or that we should benefit above all others by having agreeable ones just because we are born with what is termed a 'way with animals'. I believe that most owners who really wish to co-operate can get on the right terms with their animals. Those, on the other hand, who deliberately spoil their animals, certainly deserve all they get. An animal despises a spineless and too indulgent owner – as someone said to me the other day, animals are accustomed to taking commands from their herd or pack leader, and in many cases this instinct is the one that exists between master and dog, the master being the substitute for the leader. I have mentioned this relationship already, but it is not the only possibility, for I think animals can evidence a much purer love than that; and to me their wishes are solely governed by their love and respect for their owner, respect that comes from being properly trained and taught to obey necessary commands, and by so doing making it possible to live in close contact with their owner. A horse that shares its master's work or play, or lives with him for long hours as mine did in the Argentine, and is talked to and treated with sympathy and love, must develop a higher intelligence and faithfulness than one that is treated as though it were just a bicycle.

People ask if the breathing up the nose has the same effect on a dog as it does on a horse? Of course it has not, because dogs know friend or foe by scent. Practically everything in a dog's life is governed primarily by this instinct. We humans all have very distinctive scents for good or ill, and dogs know instantly whether to love you or not as they sniff at your hand or shoe. I always allow a dog to sniff me before making any approach to him; then, having been accepted, I gain his respect by being firm in my commands, exciting in the tone of voice I use if I want him to be interested, or soft and sympathetic if he is nervous. I know he must sense the great love I have for all dogs, and I caress him with extreme gentleness, using more of a smoothing gesture than a pat. I always gently scratch the chest of a new dog friend, or if I wish to praise a dog, and it has a most soothing effect.

I believe one has to give a great deal of onself to animals if one is to get the best out of them. And, what is more, one has to treat them as one would like to be treated oneself. If we are to get the best out of our dogs, it is no good shutting them up in kennels for the greater part of their lives, and then expecting them to be intelligent when they come out. In my opinion animals must live with one constantly, and learn words and thoughts that one says and transmits, if they are to be true companions. I never order my dog to do things, I just ask her if she would like to shut the door for her mistress, or do whatever I want, and she instantly complies with evident pleasure.

With horses I think the affection and natural obedience they have for us humans is more selfless than are the dog's. After all, a horse gets little else beyond attention to its daily needs, and being occasionally talked to and ridden, but a dog shares (if he has a good home) all the ups and down of the life of the household. By being particularly enchanting in his way he often gets a titbit, or a game of ball, or an exciting walk, and he well knows how to melt his owner's heart. How often have I, even when really ill, staggered out onto the common for the dog's walk rather than let those beautiful brown eyes see that I don't really want to go. I always feel that, as far as is humanly possible, animals should never be let down, if one is to have their whole-hearted affection. The dog that never knows at what time he is to go for a walk or have his meal, searches his pleasure elsewhere.

All animals live by clockwork timing; if fed regularly, their saliva starts to run at the appointed mealtime and one hardly needs a clock to live by. You should just hear the plaintive noise my cows make if I am late for milking, and the look of sad reproach they give me as I arrive! If I am early, and in a hurry, they will then hold back their milk and pay me out by going down in yield. Animals certainly give one enormous pleasure, but one tends to become a slave to them, and one's life has to be ruled according to their needs.

'Talking to Animals' isn't a matter of words used, it is a matter of your thoughts, your expression, and above all the tone of your voice. A harsh voice from me can make my cows jump in terror. I shouted at old Queenie once and she got such a shock that she fell down just as if she'd been shot, making me very ashamed of myself – but animals *can* be annoying sometimes! A horse doesn't need the harsh words 'get over' in the stable; a whispered command is all it wants. A horse's hearing is very acute and I, for one, never speak to a horse in anything but a whisper, or my 'little voice' that I keep for animals or tiny babies. Should a horse deliberately disobey, then a harsh voice should be sufficient to put terror into his mind to prevent him from repeating his offence.

When I speak of 'expression' I really do mean that animals watch to see whether one's face is smiling or dull. If I don't smile at my dog, whilst she is working in the obedience tests, she fails hopelessly, just as when training her I used to look sad when she did wrong, and that hurt her. Incidentally, it is quite funny to see her face sometimes, for she has learnt to smile by wrinkling up her eyes exactly as I do – on the other hand my daughter's little dog smiles properly by showing all her teeth. Dogs copy their owners, and perhaps that is why people say we become like our dogs.

One of the wonderful things about a dog, it seems to me, is that it never bears a grudge if one gets angry, and a kind word is enough to make the dog rapturously happy again. Human beings so often sulk for days if one has offended them. I remember some years back going to see an old farmer, and his wife said he was out in the cowshed, but ought to have been in by now. I went out to find him, and there he was fast asleep with his bucket still under the cow, his head resting gently on the cow's flank, and she in her patient way keeping quite still chewing her cud. I don't know how long he'd have stayed there if I hadn't turned up, but I wondered whether it was the quest for peace, perfect peace, away from his overbearing wife, that made him seek refuge and a rest with his beloved animals. I find that my own visits to my cows and horses also always have a soothing effect on me. One has to move and speak gently when one is with animals and doing that naturally makes one relax.

When I was a tiny child I used to watch my mother surreptitiously, when her maid was brushing her hair, which was of a pure spun gold, not red or fair, just gold and very long. Every day I would watch it being brushed until it shone, and then off I would go to brush the tail of the rocking horse. My old pony from Wyoming, poor wretched animal, had a docked tail, and he was tortured by flies, poor old thing, so I used vainly to brush the wisp on the end of his tail for hours on end, trying to make it longer. If love could have achieved marvels that tail would have grown again! Later on, when I had horses with long tails and manes, I gave them the most loving attention, not a hair being left unbrushed, and people used to admire the way they were tidied up and brushed until they shone. During the war, when soapflakes were scarce, never once did I miss washing my cows' beautiful tails also, and brushing them out into thick bushes at the ends. They used nearly to reach the ground and I am sure that many a cow of mine fetched a higher price than it would have done ordinarily, because it looked so beautiful with its shining coat and its well-brushed tail. It always seems to me such a shame that people who have animals should not give them a chance of keeping clean – pigs in particular, for there is no cleaner animal when properly housed. Mine always have a warm bed at one end of their shed, and never by any chance do they soil their bedding. And there is nothing a pig loves more than a good bath, with a loofah and plenty of soapflakes – although that perhaps is an unusual luxury – but there is something delightfully lovable about a really clean pig, in clean yellow straw, and it always grieves me to see the way they are kept more often than not.

Some readers may wonder why, in this book, I have made no mention of cats. I have certainly had some lovely cats in my time, but tragedy seems usually to have ended their lives. My first was a little black stray I called Sinner, that I had when I was a child. He slept down at the foot of my bed and always woke me gently at five o'clock in the morning, when he thought it was time to get up. He would creep very quietly up to my face and breathe near my nose, and I wonder whether other people have found their cats behaving like this, and whether it is a greeting of friendship as it is with horses? Sinner went everywhere with me: if I was playing in the garden he would be hiding in the bushes nearby, or lying asleep in the sun within hearing distance, and it was this trick of following me about, but of seldom letting me see him doing it, that finally cost him his life, for he rushed after me into the road and was run over.

But we seldom had cats as children, for Nanny had a horror of their jumping up onto her back. Since then, however, I have seldom been without one; but of those that I have had, three got stolen from me in quick succession, and I wondered anxiously what had become of them. But one day, alas, I finally knew, for one poor thing came home absolutely stinking of cat and urine – he must have been caught for the vile fur trade and have escaped from the sack after having been confined with others. After that episode, it was a long time before I kept another cat, since it seemed to me that, if that was to be their fate where we lived, then it was not fair to keep one at all, for one cannot confine a cat to the house in the way that one can a dog.

At the present time I possess a stray cat, who lives dangerously in the barns and fields and hedges. She comes in for her food twice a day, but disdains the suggestion that she should come to live in the house. She hunts everything, in the cruel way of her species, but still condescends to accompany me on my walks with the dogs, which is unusual. She never stays with us for long, but just bounds out at us from the hedgerow at intervals, which goes to support my theory that the cat is a creature that is well satisfied with its independence of man. But many generations of mankind have certainly worshipped at its shrine, and it accepts man's favours if they are offered – perhaps, just as a token of respect! There is no denying that many cats tolerate the warmth and take the hearth of man as their birthright, but they always seem to reserve to themselves the right to disappear at any time to follow their private pursuits, without ever a farewell to their owner. In my own lifetime I think I have worried more over the temporary disappearance of my cats than about anything else. But one always forgives them at once, when they come back with tails held aloft, and with soft purring to dispel any anger that might be forthcoming. If you *must* keep a cat, you will have to be prepared to play second fiddle to it, which most cat-owners don't refuse to do. Yet, if your life is one of sacrifice to your cat's wishes, you will receive abundant love, although you must never deceive yourself into imagining that your cat will become your slave – you yourself will always remain the slave of your cat. They certainly were not worshipped in ancient Egypt just to become the slaves of this modern world!

This is perhaps the appropriate place to say just a little more about my method of training Archie. As I mentioned on page 31, my frequent command to him was 'Canter at the third tree'. This was not my way of presenting a mathematical problem to be worked out by Archie, nor was it in this case an exercise depending on intonation of voice; it was taught, as most orders are taught to animals, by constant repetition and reward. When he was a beginner at the job, I would tell the pupil that I would make Archie canter at the third tree and then walk at the fifth tree; I did so by calling out the word 'canter', which of course all my horses know after I have had them a few hours, then he would get used to the 'third tree' idea, the words being connected with my command to canter. In the end he needed no command at all: for he had learnt to connect the third tree with the 'canter' command. He now knew perfectly the basic commands 'canter', 'walk', or 'trot', the place for doing them having been repeated so often in the same routine daily that he could have done it blindfold. In exactly the same way a milkman's horse knows where his customers live, or a guide-dog knows the normal journeys of its owner. Once an animal is taught something, it has a perfect memory for sequences. This is why a riding-school horse can be relied on to carry out commands when it has beginners on its back.

We all have our likes and dislikes in the animal kingdom : some people choose queer beasts as pets and find great joy in their strange friends; some even liking snakes or alligators, which would certainly not appeal to me. But I expect they could tell you all about their strange habits and ways they have of communicating with human beings, for I believe there is a language for every species of animal, bird, and reptile, if you study it long enough, and many are the stories one hears of people who can talk to birds, or even to wolves. But I feel that no matter what language is spoken, the same principles underlie everything. The talk, whatever its form, must be based upon a great love, a great desire to be real friends with the animal, and, above all, on complete freedom from fear. The love of animals and other creatures is a bond all human beings have with each other whatever race or creed theirs may be, and I am sure the little Russian boy cries over the loss of his pet just as bitterly as the little English boy over his lost mouse.

Where animal lovers meet there is a common language and understanding. Christ chose a donkey to ride on, in the knowledge that the most humble of animals was worthy to serve him. If we love and talk to animals in such a way that our love is transmitted to them, they are waiting to serve us, I am sure.

> 'Tis sweet to hear the watch-dog's honest bark
> Bay deep-mouthed welcome as we draw near home;
> 'Tis sweet to know there is an eye will mark
> Our coming, and look brighter when we come.
>
> *Don Juan*, Canto I, St. 123.

Fontana New Naturalist

This series, edited by John Gilmour, Sir Julian Huxley, Margaret Davies and Kenneth Mellanby, was originally published by Collins. The Fontana paperback editions comprise:

The Snowdonia National Park William Condry **75p**

The Highlands and Islands F. Fraser Darling and J. Morton Boyd **60p**

The Peak District K. C. Edwards **60p**

A Natural History of Man in Britain H. J. Fleure and M. Davies **75p**

The Trout W. E. Frost and M. E. Brown **60p**

Wild Flowers J. Gilmour and M. Walters **60p**

The Open Sea: Its Natural History
Part One: The World of Plankton
Sir Alister Hardy **90p**

Insect Natural History A. D. Imms **80p**

The Life of the Robin David Lack **40p**

Life in Lakes and Rivers
T. T. Macan and E. B. Worthington **60p**

Climate and the British Scene Gordon Manley **75p**

Pesticides and Pollution Kenneth Mellanby **45p**

Mountains and Moorlands W. H. Pearsall **60p**

The World of the Soil Sir E. John Russell **50p**

Britain's Structure and Scenery L. Dudley Stamp **60p**

The Sea Shore C. M. Yonge **60p**

A Fontana Selection

Ideology in Social Science, edited by Robin Blackburn

Stonehenge Decoded, Gerald S. Hawkins

Romantic Image, Frank Kermode

Memories, Dreams, Reflections, C. G. Jung

The Dominant Man, Humphry Knipe and George Maclay

Reformation Europe (1517-1559), G. R. Elton

Social Problems in Modern Britain,
  edited by Eric Butterworth and David Weir

The Screwtape Letters, C. S. Lewis

My Early Life, Winston Churchill

Voyage to Atlantis, James W. Mavor

The First Four Georges, J. H. Plumb

Natural History of Man in Britain, H. J. Fleure and M. Davies

Waiting on God, Simone Weil

The Wandering Scholars, Helen Waddell

Italian Painters of the Renaissance, Bernhard Berenson